HOPE TO WIN –
PREPARE TO APPEAL
and change the law along the way

JERRY H. SUMMERS

Waldenhouse Publishers, Inc.
Walden, Tennessee

Hope to Win – Prepare to Appeal: and change the law along the way
Copyright 2022© Jerry H. Summers 1941. All rights reserved. No part of this book may be reproduced in any form or by any electronic or mechanical means including information storage and retrieval systems, without permission in writing from the publisher. The only exception is by a reviewer, who may quote short excerpts in a review.
Published by Waldenhouse Publishers, Inc.
100 Clegg Street, Signal Mountain, Tennessee 37377 USA
423-886-2721 www.waldenhouse.com
Printed in the United States of America
Type and Design by Karen Paul Stone
ISBN: 978-1-947589-55-1
Library of Congress Control Number: 2022943566
Combines an introduction to law and an examination of constitutional principles at the core of the American justice system as viewed by an experienced trial attorney for aspiring young lawyers. Employs more than two dozen state and federal cases as examples; includes question and answer format. – provided by Publisher
LAW000000   LAW / General
LAW026000   LAW / Criminal Law / General
LAW026020   LAW / Criminal Law / Sentencing

Proceeds from the sale of *Hope to Win, Prepare to Appeal* are donated to the Summers, Rufolo, and Rodgers Trial Advocacy Endowment, Center for Advocacy and Dispute Resolution, University of Tennessee College of Law through the University of Tennessee Foundation (UTF), 1525 University Avenue, Knoxville, TN 37921-4848. UTF is a charitable, non-profit corporation.
Donations should be made to University of Tennessee Foundation Inc. for the Summers, Rufolo, and Rodgers Trial Advocacy Endowment.

DEDICATION

I dedicate this book

To all those attorneys and aspiring attorneys who appreciate that in America we must conduct a legal revolution in the courts challenging unfair and often unconstitutional statutes and precedents;

To all those who are willing to fight unjust results and swim upstream against adverse decisions by the courts;

To those who are persistent, recognizing that many of the leading decisions that protect the constitutional rights of individuals came only after the same arguments had been made, unsuccessfully, over and over;

To those who are creative and tireless, working to distinguish their cases from adverse precedents;

To those who despite public sentiment undertake to assure that everyone has the right to counsel in both civil and criminal cases;

And, importantly, to law students who will be inspired to continue the legal revolution in the future.

JERRY SUMMERS, 2022

TABLE OF CONTENTS

PREFACE

When I entered the practice of law on September 1, 1966, as a young inexperienced prosecutor with the Hamilton County District Attorney's Office, challenges to unfair practices in criminal law and criminal procedure were increasing, with increased attention being paid to protecting individuals' constitutional rights in the federal court system. The United States Supreme Court was at the forefront of that revolution. Tennessee, on the other hand, was reluctant to adopt many of the progressive decisions of the Court up in Washington D.C., until 1974, when the "Great Supreme Court" of Tennessee, which included Justice William Fones of Memphis, Justice William Harbison of Nashville, Justice Joe Henry of Pulaski, Justice Robert Cooper, Sr. of Chattanooga, and Justice Ray Brock, Jr. of Chattanooga, were elected to the Tennessee Supreme Court.

Justices Henry and Brock were experienced trial lawyers and were in favor of changing the Tennessee Supreme Court's direction with respect to protecting the rights of the accused. Justice Harbison was credited with being one of the brightest legal minds to graduate from Vanderbilt Law School in Nashville and was a known conservative. Justice Robert Cooper had been an assistant district attorney in Hamilton County prior to being appointed to the Circuit Court (1953-1960) and Tennessee Court of Appeals (1960-1974). Justice Fones from Memphis was the only holdover from the prior Court which had been replaced by the Democratic Executive Committee in an open meeting in Nashville. Several politicians questioned Justice Fones' political alliance as a Democrat, but he was approved after convincing the party that he was a loyal member.

Until 1974, the only step forward in protecting the rights of the accused that had occurred in Tennessee was the application of the constitutional requirements of *Miranda v. Arizona*, 384 U.S. 436 (1966) in the Tennessee case of *Shannon v. State*, 427 S.W.2d 26 (Tenn. 1968), discussed in Chapter I in this book. I was the young Assistant District Attorney who was responsible for the application of *Miranda* in our state. Although my boss, District Attorney General Edward E. Davis, is reported as having tried the case for the prosecution, he actually did not participate in the trial. Former Assistant District Attorney (and future Hamilton County Criminal Court Judge) Douglas A. Meyer raised the issue in the trial court. Perhaps because it was potentially a controversial decision, when the Tennessee Supreme Court embraced the *Miranda* guidelines, they did so via a per curiam opinion, which meant that the opinion was agreed to by all members of the court and issued in the name of the court, so one would not bear political fallout for writing the opinion in the event of a negative reaction.

I learned a valuable lesson early in my legal career. A trial lawyer should not readily accept as precedent a decision that, when applied to the specific facts of your case, renders an unfair result. Instead, counsel should attack the precedent, or the statute or policy, asserting the fundamental right to a fair trial, which is guaranteed under both the United States and Tennessee Constitution. In this way, a lawyer does not inadvertently waive a federal claim should the case end up in federal court.

Hopefully, the cases discussed in this book demonstrate how to raise issues, preserve errors for appellate review, and differentiate bad precedent when arguing against the application of the doctrine of "stare decisis," which requires that, as a general rule, courts stand by their prior decisions. You will find a good example of this tactic in the case of *In re Brock*, 536 S.W. 3d 409 (Tenn. 2017), discussed in Chapter XXIV. In *Brock*, the Tennessee Supreme Court overruled a 1905 case, resulting in a significant settlement in a case involving a substantial will contest.

When I started a draft of this book,
I wanted to accomplish two things:

(1) To use my fifty-six years of experience as a trial lawyer to motivate law students and lawyers to fight for changes in the law and to challenge unfair practices that may be the product of a politically-motivated General Assembly or similarly motivated trial and appellate courts; and

(2) To provide a teaching tool about trial and appellate practice for law students, while raising additional funding for the scholarships

annually awarded to third-year students by the Center for Advocacy and Dispute Resolution at the University of Tennessee College of Law.

I hope the lessons I have learned and write about in this book will be of help to practicing lawyers and those who will represent clients in future generations.

ACKNOWLEDGMENTS

Many individuals and organizations have contributed to the end results in many of the cases in this book. They deserve some of the credit for any public interest this publication generates.

My first case in the United States Supreme Court in 1973, *Brooks vs. Tennessee,* dealt with the constitutionality of a Tennessee statute that required the defendant to be the first witness for the defense; otherwise, the defendant would be prevented from testifying. University of Tennessee law student, Charles "Chuck" Dupree of Chattanooga prepared a memo for me on the issue and it formed the initial basis for the appeal.

Throughout the years I have had excellent attorneys who helped me with briefs, motions, and appeals in the cases mentioned in this book as well as many other unmentioned cases.

Sandy McCrea was a law clerk for the late revered federal Judge Frank W. Wilson and chose not to follow the usual course of going to work for a big law firm in Chattanooga. Instead, she came to work for me, and for at least fifteen years, she was an invaluable asset and helped on appeals and in the courtroom.

Marya Schalk came into our firm upon the recommendation of retired Tennessee Court of Criminal Appeals Judge Joe Tipton after she had clerked for him following her graduation from the University of Tennessee College of Law. She has been instrumental in making certain that the sometimes crazy and controversial positions I have taken in these and others cases have been in proper legal form.

Attorneys Cahill Hitt, Tom Harris, and Jim Robinson of Chattanooga were gracious co-counsel in their cases mentioned in this book and have to be recognized as contributing much toward the favorable final results obtained.

The Tennessee Associational of Criminal Defense Lawyers (TACDL) allowed me to file amicus curiae briefs in some cases and supported me by lending their prestige to these cases. TACDL is a group of over one thousand members who strive to protect the constitutional rights of persons accused of crimes in Tennessee.

I would be remiss if I didn't mention the various lawyers who have been with me over the years I have been in practice. Ed Love, Judge John McClarty, Sandy McCrea, Judge Tom Wright, Judge Tom Wyatt, Jeff Rufolo, Jimmy Rodgers, Jr., Judge Tom Greenholtz, Chris Dixon, Marya Schalk and Ben McGowan are all great lawyers and have tolerated and supported me in my "lost causes," which fortunately sometimes resulted in the reversal of a conviction and/or changed an unfair procedure.

To them and our support staff of secretaries, paralegals, and runners, I am eternally grateful. Nick Walker and Joy Hayes get special credit for their typing of the drafts of this work. Finally to Marya who took on the task of correcting my many mistakes in this book I say thank you — again!

I also would like to thank Professor Penny White and the students in the Advocacy and Dispute Resolution Concentration at the University of Tennessee College of Law for their expertise in preparing the "Q & A" and "What I Know" portions of the book.

If I have omitted others whom I should have recognized, the omission was inadvertent and I apologize.

INTRODUCTION

Between 1968 and 2018, I have tried many cases in both the civil and criminal courts. The several cases that are mentioned herein are not the only ones I have lost (or won) but constitute an array of decisions, in a variety of legal contexts, where I have been able to change the law or, at a minimum, expose an illegal practice, even if I ultimately lost the case. I offer the stories of these cases to those who want to be lawyers to demonstrate the opportunities that come from being a lawyer; to young lawyers to inspire them to challenge bad laws, bad policies, and bad practices; and to more seasoned lawyers to encourage them to continue to put their clients first and to find time to mentor young lawyers in an effort to improve our justice system for all.

After graduating from the University of the South in 1963, I was awarded one of seven freshman scholarships to the University of Tennessee College of Law at Knoxville. I immediately proceeded to lose the scholarship and almost flunk out of law school. I was not named to Order of the Coif (legal honor for those with the highest grades); I never made Law Review. I often say I was in the one percent of my class, "the one percent that held up the other ninety-nine percent!"

Some people mistakenly consider me to be a constitutional lawyer, but to merit such distinction, you really do have to make better than a "D" in constitutional law. When I graduated from law school in 1966, the only accomplishment that I could brag about was a second-place finish with co-counsel, John Murray, in the College's annual moot court competition. But, it was that result that gave me hope that I might be able to make it as a trial lawyer.

In spite of all this, I was able to graduate, pass the bar, and with the help of an aunt and uncle by marriage, I got a job as an assistant district attorney with a good salary and the opportunity to learn in the best teaching facility for an aspiring trial lawyer — the courtroom. I learned valuable lessons during my twenty-eight months as a prosecutor, which still help me today in the twilight years of my practice. Hopefully some of the lessons I have learned trying cases will benefit up and coming trial lawyers.

Even the best prepared and most astute trial lawyer cannot win every case. When a lawyer loses in the trial court, the lawyer may want to ask an appellate court to overrule the trial judge, but in order to do that, the lawyer must have "made a record." In other words, the lawyer must have objected and placed sufficient information in the trial court record for the appellate court to understand the issue.

Many of the cases in this book illustrate how a bad result in the trial court was corrected by an appellate court; others show how we convinced an appellate court to reconsider and modify bad precedent; still others demonstrate how change in the law can be motivated by exposing and challenging unfair policies even when a case is lost in court.

The theme of this publication is simple: "Hope to win, prepare to appeal." I have used this strategy for more than fifty-six years not out of disbelief in my clients' causes, but because of my sincere belief that when trial court decisions and legislative enactments do not honor the right to a fair trial, a detached appellate court may listen to your argument more impartially. Politics, public opinion, media coverage, and sensational high profile cases put substantial pressure on local trial court judges, particularly in election years. The saying that "the best politicians make the worst judges and the best judges make the worst politicians" has a certain amount of validity! I have found it is sometimes easier to convince an appellate court, detached from the local pressures, to "take the blame" for an unpopular decision. But unless the record is preserved, the appellate court will not be able to cure the error.

Hopefully, this book will inspire trial lawyers – young and old – to challenge unreasonable practices, unjust precedent, and unfair laws at trial, but to always build a record and be prepared to appeal!

READING AND USING THIS BOOK

Jerry Summer's eighth book is a remarkably candid description of what it means to be a trial lawyer. Indeed, it illustrates the incredible difficulties of being a trial lawyer, of losing cases you believe you should have won, of representing people who others despise, of knowing that decisions are being reached based on reasons other than the law and the facts. But the book does far more than describe the difficulties, it confirms the benefit of tenacity, commitment, and courage.

The book is an inspirational read for lawyers, young and old alike, because it not only prepares new lawyers for the complex challenges that practicing law presents, it also motivates more seasoned lawyers to maintain their commitment to their clients and to the improvement of the justice system. Moreover, the book provides great insight into the imperfections of the law and our court system, and educates others interested in the state of justice in America.

This book is easily adapted for use as a textbook for pre-law, introductory law, and first-year law classes. Most chapters revolve around a single case and the decisions the case prompted in the state and federal courts. Each chapter includes a historical, factual, and legal framework. To stimulate thought about particular aspects of substantive law and procedure, each chapter is preceded by a series of questions, "Q & A," for the student (or reader) to consider before reading the chapter. After reading the chapter and, perhaps, following a class discussion, the student may return to the Q & A and then compare their conclusions with the answers provided in the "What I Know" section at the end of each chapter. Both the "Q & A" and the "What I Know" sections were largely the work of second-year law students, who have recently mastered the topics themselves as students in the Advocacy and Dispute Resolution Concentration at the UT College of Law.

The breadth of the substantive and procedural issues raised provides a comprehensive introduction to the study of law and the justice system, while the candor and humility of Jerry Summers' approach gives keen insight into what it really means to be a trial lawyer.

It is impossible to read this book and not come away knowing that a single lawyer who demonstrates boldness, determination, and resilience can truly make a difference in the lives of others – many others.

The students in the Center for Advocacy and Dispute Resolution are grateful to Jerry Summers for writing this book and for giving them an opportunity to provide input through the "Q & A" and "What I Know" sections of each chapter. The contributing students are listed below. All are entitled to recognition, but special recognition goes to Benjamin Barker, a Tennessee Law Scholar, who put in extra effort in assuring the high quality of the students' input.

Meghan Alderson
Benjamin Barker
Lilly Anna Fairweather
Meghan Alderson
Keelin Kraemer
Penny White, Director, Center for
    Advocacy and Dispute Resolution, 2022

Chapter I
Shannon v. State, 427 S.W.2d 26 (1968)

1. Think about the dynamics that are present when a police officer questions an individual.[1] How do those dynamics change when the individual is in police custody?[2]

2. Should an individual have the right to have an attorney present when being questioned by police? Why or why not?

3. What constitutional rights apply when an individual is in police custody?

4. How do those constitutional rights impact police questioning?

5. What is a voluntary and involuntary confession?

6. What is the *Miranda* rule?

7. What is the "exclusionary rule?"

8. What is the "fruit of the poisonous tree" doctrine?

---

1. The process of questioning of an individual by a police officer is generally referred to as "interrogation."

2. Once an individual is placed in police custody, the individual is "seized" or under arrest.

CHAPTER I

SHANNON v. STATE
427 S.W.2d 26 (Tenn. 1968)

Early in my career, I served as an Assistant District Attorney, working with District Attorney General Edward E. Davis. Although I actually tried this case involving the horrible murder of an elderly lady, my name was left off the appellate decisions and replaced with his. In hindsight, I sometimes think that my zeal to get a conviction justified the omission.

On July 29, 1966, Mrs. Gunnie Lasley was murdered at her home on Green Pond Road in Daisy, Hamilton County, Tennessee. Her death was caused by stab wounds and skull fractures.

Mrs. Lasley's body was allegedly found by the defendant, Ed Shannon, who lived with his mother in a house between one hundred fifty and two hundred yards from the deceased's residence. Shannon was a military veteran who, after losing a leg in World War II, had been honorably discharged. At forty-three years of age, he was illiterate, an alcoholic, and lived at home with his mother.

Shannon called the police and was at Mrs. Lasley's home when the police arrived. The police collected evidence at the scene, but none of the collected evidence incriminated Shannon. Police also took Shannon into custody for questioning; because Shannon was on the verge of delirium tremors, the police gave him alcohol during the questioning. Nonetheless, Shannon gave only a non-incriminating statement and was subsequently released.

Seventeen days after the murder, Shannon was taken by police to a motel for questioning. After first declining a lie detector test, Shannon eventually took a test but was told by police that he had failed the test. He then gave a confession under doubtful circumstances. For example, Shannon was questioned for five or six hours; the officer taking the statement prompted Shannon as to what to say; and Shannon was alone during the entire interrogation, with no legal counsel, friends, or family present. When Shannon signed his confession, he also signed a waiver that stated: "I have also been told that I have the right to call a lawyer or have one called for me and have him present." *Shannon v. State*, 427 S.W.2d at 28.

When the case came for trial, defense counsel argued that Shannon's statement should be excluded from evidence because it was not voluntary. The trial judge agreed that the written statement was not a voluntary confession, finding that it was coerced by Shannon's interrogators who prompted the statement by claiming he had failed to pass a lie detector test.

Although this written statement was not admitted into evidence at trial, the trial judge allowed two later statements made by Shannon to be presented to the jury. One of the admitted statements was made during booking, when Shannon reportedly told the booking officer that when Mrs. Lasley made a comment about a woman who Shannon had lived with, he "got all up in the air about it and when he came to she was on the floor dead." *Id.* The second statement was in reaction to being shown one of the knives used in the killing. Ultimately, Shannon was convicted of second-degree murder.

When Shannon's appeal reached the Tennessee Supreme Court, it gave that court an early opportunities to apply protections outlined two years earlier by the United States Supreme Court in *Miranda* v. Arizona, 384 U.S. 436 (1966). The *Miranda* decision prohibited the use of statements made by one in custody who was questioned by police without first being advised (or "warned") of important constitutional rights including the right to remain silent and the right to have court-appointed counsel. Because the *Miranda* rule applied in state and federal courts, the Tennessee Supreme Court had to determine first whether the "warnings" police gave Shannon satisfied the *Miranda* rule.

The Tennessee Supreme Court held that the warnings given to Shannon fell "short of the plain requirement" of *Miranda*. By advising Shannon only that he had the right "to call a lawyer or have one called for [him] and have him present," the police failed to advise Shannon that he was entitled to have an attorney appointed even if he could not afford an attorney. *Shannon v. State*, 427 S.W.2d at 28-29. Thus, Shannon's written and signed statement was not admissible because the police failed to comply with the *Miranda* requirements.

Additionally, the Tennessee Supreme Court prohibited the introduction of Shannon's other two statements. They, too, were sought without giving Shannon a clear explanation of his right to counsel and were the "fruit" of the first statement and also inadmissible. *Id.* at 29.

Shannon's conviction was reversed, and the case was remanded to the trial court for a new trial. But without being able to admit the defendant's statements, the state was forced to retire the case without retrying it.

What I Know

1. Most individuals – even those who are completely law-abiding citizens – experience some level of anxiety when confronted by the police. The stress and anxiety is heightened when an individual has been placed in police custody. In fact, the United States Supreme Court has recognized that police custody creates an inherently coercive atmosphere, requiring that police follow safeguards to assure that individuals in police custody do not feel compelled to incriminate themselves.

2. The United States Supreme Court has also held that an accused has a right to have an attorney present during police questioning. The presence of the attorney helps assure that the individual is not being pressured, threatened, or intimidated and that the individual does not involuntarily or mistakenly give up the right to remain silent. Attorneys may also provide counsel and advice during police questioning, including the advice not to answer further questions.

3. When an individual is in police custody, the individual has the right (1) to remain silent, (2) to be advised that anything said can be used in court, (3) to have counsel present during questioning, (4) to have an attorney appointed if the individual cannot afford counsel.

4. The police must inform the accused of all of the constitutional rights enumerated above in advance of any questioning and must secure a knowing and intelligent waiver of those rights before questioning can begin. If an accused waives the rights and responds to questions and then chooses to invoke the right to remain silent, questioning must stop. If an accused responds to questions and then requests counsel, questioning must stop until counsel is provided.

5. A voluntary confession is one that is a product of individual free will and not obtained by force, coercion, or intimidation. An involuntary confession is one that is not given out of free will, but that is the

result of force, coercion, or intimidation. Under the law, involuntary confessions are not admissible.

6. The *Miranda* rule requires police to inform an individual who is in custody, prior to any police interrogation, of his or her constitutional rights set forth in 3 *infra*.

7. The exclusionary rule is a rule that excludes evidence or statements that are obtained improperly or illegally, usually as a result of the violation of an accused's constitutional rights. For example, if the police secure a confession from an individual who is in custody without first obtaining a waiver of the individual's *Miranda* rights, the exclusionary rule will operate to exclude the confession from evidence except in rare circumstances.

8. The "fruit of the poisonous tree" doctrine extends the exclusionary rule to evidence directly derived from or exposed through the original excluded evidence. Together, the exclusionary rule and the fruit of the poisonous tree doctrine make the rights protected by the Fourth, Fifth, and Sixth Amendments meaningful. For example, if the police secure a confession in violation of *Miranda* and, based on that confession, secure a search warrant for a home that, when executed, leads to the discovery of an illegal substance, the evidence produced by the search is the "fruit," (the result) of the "poisonous tree," (the original illegality), which in this example is the illegal interrogation.

Chapter II
Brooks v. Tennessee, 406 U.S. 605 (1972)

1. In this case, a state statute impacted a constitutional right. What is the interplay between a state law, a state constitution, and the United States Constitution?

2. What were the state constitutional rights at issue in this case?

3. How did counsel raise the constitutional issues in court?

4. What was the process by which the case moved from the local criminal court to the United States Supreme Court?

5. What does it mean for a case to be "remanded" by the United States Supreme Court?

6. How did the "win" in the United States Supreme Court impact the final resolution of Brooks' case?

7. What impact did counsel's work in this case have on other cases?

CHAPTER II

BROOKS v. TENNESSEE
406 U.S. 605 (1972)

After leaving the District Attorney's office, I began my career as a criminal defense lawyer, a career that would allow me to appear in state and federal courts on behalf of hundreds of individuals. More than once, I had the distinct honor of taking a case to the United States Supreme Court. The first of those cases was *Brooks v. Tennessee,* a case that overturned a long-standing unconstitutional law in the state of Tennessee.

My client, Donald Brooks, was charged in the Criminal Court for Hamilton County, Tennessee with armed robbery and unlawful possession of a weapon. After the prosecution had put on its case, we requested to delay defendant's testimony until after other defense witnesses had testified. Although Tennessee law at the time required a defendant who wished to testify to testify before any other defense testimony,[1] the prosecutor agreed to waive the provisions of the law, but the trial judge, the Honorable Campbell Carden, refused to accept the waiver stating, "The law is, as you know it to be, that if a defendant testifies, he has to testify first." 406 U.S. at 606.

The State's case against our client was strong, but we questioned the validity of the judge's ruling. In order to raise that issue, the defense took a "Hail Mary" approach, questioning the validity of the law. In order to preserve the issue for appellate review, the defense called two witnesses, but the defendant himself did not testify.

Brooks was convicted and we appealed to the Tennessee Court of Criminal Appeals, arguing that the Tennessee statute that we had challenged violated the state and federal Constitutions. When we lost

---

1. The statute in question, Tennessee Code Annotated Section 40-2403, was first enacted in 1887, and provided that defendants in criminal cases could testify on their own behalf but must do so before any other testimony offered by the defense.

that appeal, we sought an appeal to the Tennessee Supreme Court, which denied review.[2]

We believed that our constitutional challenge was valid, despite the longstanding practice in Tennessee. We filed a petition for writ of certiorari in the United States Supreme Court, a long shot for any defendant convicted in state court.[3] But our approach paid off! In a decision by Justice Brennan, notwithstanding dissents by Chief Justice Burger and Justices Blackmun and Rehnquist, the Court held that the Tennessee statute violated due process and the privilege against self-incrimination. By forcing an accused to testify first, or not at all, the law burdened the fundamental right to remain silent and the right to counsel's guidance in determining not only whether an accused should testify, but also when.

Brooks' conviction was reversed, and the case remanded for a new trial. When the case came back, we were able to resolve the case on reduced charges.

---

2. While a convicted defendant has an automatic right to appeal to the Tennessee Court of Criminal Appeals, an appeal to the Tennessee Supreme Court, in all but death penalty cases, must be granted by the Tennessee Supreme Court.

3. To secure a review in the United States Supreme Court, a party must file a petition for writ of certiorari, which, when translated, means "to be made certain." The petition must convince the Court of the importance of accepting the case, outlining the federal rights at issue. The United States Supreme Court grants certiorari in state cases only when important federal constitutional rights are involved.

What I Know

1. The United States Constitution provides that the United States Constitution is the supreme law of the land. U.S. Const. Art. VI, clause 2. While state constitutions and laws can provide greater rights to individuals than that provided by the federal constitution, neither can interfere with an individual's rights as protected by the United States Constitution.

2. In this case, the constitutional rights at issue were the defendant's right to be free from self-incrimination and the right to due process of law.

3. Counsel raised the federal constitutional issues in the state trial court by filing a motion that challenged the constitutionality of the state law and requested that the accused be allowed to testify after other defense witnesses. In other words, counsel argued that the state law violated the federal constitutional rights of the accused.

4. This case originated in the Hamilton County Criminal Court. From there, it was appealed as of right to the Tennessee Court of Criminal Appeals; then, permission to appeal was requested and denied by the Tennessee Supreme Court. Subsequently, review was sought in and granted by the United States Supreme Court.

5. When the United States Supreme Court "remands" a case to a lower court that means that the case is being sent back to the lower court for final resolution, consistent with the decision reached by the Supreme Court.

6. Once the United States Supreme Court ruled that the Tennessee law was unconstitutional, the State was willing to negotiate and eventually settle the case on reduced charges, likely because of the amount of time, energy, and money that had already been expended in the case.

7. Counsel's work resulted in the state law being declared unconstitutional. Thus, the decision of the United States Supreme Court had the impact of nullifying the Tennessee statute that required the accused to testify first, if at all. The law had no further effect in Tennessee, leaving all defendants free to determine whether to testify and, if so, when to testify in the defense case.

Chapter III
Robinson v. Neil, 409 U.S. 505 (1973)

1. What does "precedent" mean?

2. When does the United States Supreme Court precedent apply to state courts?

3. What does it mean to apply precedent retroactively?

4. What is the constitutional protection against double jeopardy?

5. What do sovereignty, separate sovereignty, and dual sovereignty mean?

CHAPTER III

ROBINSON v. NEIL
409 U.S. 505 (1973)

A year later after my success in *Brooks v. State*, see Chapter II *supra*, I was asked by attorney Jim Robinson to help him get a case to the United States Supreme Court. This case originated more than a decade earlier, in 1962, when Samuel Ed Robinson was tried, convicted, and fined fifty dollars by the City Court for Chattanooga on three charges of assault and battery. This was pursuant to the long-standing practice of the city court judges to resolve cases on lesser charges, using city ordinances, in order to raise revenue for the city. Robinson was later indicted for three charges of assault with intent to commit murder, arising out of the same circumstances. When Robinson admitted his guilt, he was sentenced by the Criminal Court of Hamilton Country to three consecutive sentences ranging from three to ten years.

While incarcerated, Robinson unsuccessfully sought to set aside his conviction and sentence claiming that he had been convicted and sentenced twice for the same offenses in violation of the Double Jeopardy Clause. Both the state and federal trial courts denied Robinson's claims for habeas corpus relief and the United States Court of Appeals for the Sixth Circuit upheld the denial of his claim.[1] *Robinson v. Henderson*, 268 F. Supp. 349 (E.D. Tenn. 1967), *aff'd*, 391 F.2d 933 (6th Cir. 1968).

When the United States Supreme Court decided *Waller v. Florida*, 397 U.S. 387 (1970),[2] Robinson again filed for relief in the federal court, arguing that the decision in *Waller* required reversal of his sec-

---

1. When an incarcerated individual files a petition for a writ of habeas corpus, the individual is asserting that the confinement is illegal. The phrase "habeas corpus" literally translates to "you have the body" and when the writ of habeas corpus is granted, the warden of the prison where the individual is held is ordered to release the individual from the unlawful confinement.

ond convictions. The Chief Judge of the United States District Court for the Eastern District of Tennessee, the Honorable Frank W. Wilson, appointed attorney James (Jim) D. Robinson (no relation to defendant Robinson), of the long-established Chattanooga firm, Goins, Gammon, Baker, and Robinson to represent Robinson. The firm primarily handled the defense of insurance claims in automobile and medical malpractice cases and did not do criminal defense work.[3]

The issue for the federal court was whether the *Waller* decision was to be applied retroactively to cases that predated the decision. Judge Wilson held that the *Waller* decision was to be applied retroactively and that retroactive application required that Robinson's convictions be set aside, *Robinson v. Neil*, 320 F. Supp. 894 (E.D. Tenn. 1971), but the federal appellate court reversed. *Robinson v. Neil*, 452 F.2d 370 (6th Cir. 1971).

When Attorney Robinson asked me to help with defendant Robinson's case, he asked me to argue the case before the United States Supreme Court. Because I had received two grants of certiorari from the Court that year,[4] and had successfully argued the *Brooks* case the previous year, I may have been overconfident in believing that I would have many other opportunities to argue in the future. In addition, I was aware that arguing a case in the Supreme Court is an honor achieved by very few lawyers and that this case might be Jim Robinson's only chance to participate in an oral argument. I suggested that he present the case to the nine justices. He did the argument and did an excellent job.

---

2. The issue in *Waller* was whether an individual could be prosecuted in both state and municipal courts for a single crime arising from the same conduct. The United States Supreme Court held that the federal constitutional prohibition against double jeopardy prevented the state and municipal court from being treated as separate sovereigns. Thus, dual prosecutions were not allowed. *Waller v. United States*, 397 U.S. 387 (1970).

3. This case arose before the creation of a public defender system in the State of Tennessee and is an example of the ability of prepared and diligent lawyers to handle all types of cases.

4. The second case on which the Supreme Court had granted certiorari was *Day & Zimmerman Inc. v. Challoner*, 423 U.S. 3 (1975), a case on which I served as trial counsel with Cahill Hitt of Texarkana, Texas. That case was successfully concluded for our client in 1975 in a per curiam opinion. I have not received another grant of certiorari from the United States Supreme Court, although my office has made other attempts.

On January 13, 1973, the Supreme Court ended Samuel Ed Robinson's long battle for freedom, reversing his convictions and holding that the city and state prosecutions based on the same set of facts violated the prohibition against double jeopardy, giving the decision in *Waller* full retroactive effect.[5]

5. The opinion was written by Justice William Rehnquist and approved by the other eight justices.

What I Know

1. The word "precedent" refers to a legal decision that binds future decisions with the same or substantially similar facts.

2. Only United States Supreme Court precedent that interprets provisions of the United States Constitution that apply to states are binding on state courts. United States Supreme Court precedent interpreting federal statutes may be persuasive, in some circumstances, but is not binding in any way.

3. When a court applies precedent retroactively, the court is directing lower courts to apply the decision to other cases, including those that were decided before the precedent.

4. The Fifth Amendment to the Constitution protects against double jeopardy. In short, the protection against double jeopardy means that an individual may not be tried or punished more than once for the same criminal offense. As a result of the double jeopardy prohibition, an individual who is acquitted or convicted may not be tried again by the same sovereign. *See* 5 *infra*. Additionally, an individual who has been punished for an offense cannot be punished again by the same sovereign for the same offense.

5. "Sovereignty" refers to the power and authority of government within its borders to govern itself. "Separate sovereignty" is used to refer to the situation in which different governments derive power from different sources. For example, the federal government derives its power from the federal constitution and federal laws, while state governments derive their power from the state constitution and state laws. Thus, the federal and state governments are separate sovereigns. The United States Supreme Court has applied the doctrine of "dual sovereignty," used interchangeably with the phrase "separate sovereignty," consistently to allow two separate sovereigns to both exercise

sovereign power against an accused. Thus, prosecution of an accused for the same conduct by both the state and federal government does not violate double jeopardy.

Chapter IV
Cox v. City of Chattanooga, 516 S.W.2d 94 (Tenn. Ct. App.), cert. denied, (Tenn. 1974), cert. denied, 419 U.S. 833 (1974)

1. What constitutional right is at issue in this case and also in *State v. Shannon,* Chapter 1 *supra*?

2. What is the privilege against self-incrimination?

3. How was the privilege against self-incrimination at issue in this civil case?

4. What is a *Miranda* warning and what does it mean to waive *Miranda* rights?

5. Why would an attorney advise a client not to answer a police officer's questions?

CHAPTER IV

COX v. CITY OF CHATTANOOGA
516 S.W.2d 94 (Tenn. Ct. App.), *cert. denied*, (Tenn. 1974), *cert. denied*, 419 U.S. 833 (1974)

While constitutional rights are often at issue in criminal cases, they have been equally important to my clients in civil cases. This case, for example, implicated the privilege against self-incrimination, provided for by the Fifth Amendment to the United States Constitution, in a civil case in which my client, a fireman, was discharged after he refused to waive his *Miranda* rights and submit to questioning by Chattanooga police detectives.

Raymond Cox was a captain with the Chattanooga Fire Department. When Cox's name, home telephone number, and telephone numbers of the two precinct stations where Cox worked were found in a murder suspect's address book, Cox was confronted at his home by two Chattanooga detectives. Cox accompanied the officers to the Chattanooga Police Department but, when presented with the standard *Miranda* warning and asked to sign a waiver, Cox refused after consulting with his attorney. The following day, Cox was fired by the commissioner of the fire and police department for insubordination, conduct unbecoming of an officer, and refusal to cooperate with an investigation.

Cox appealed the commissioner's decision to fire him to the five-member Board of Commissioners. The Board of Commissioners upheld Cox's termination and Cox asked the chancery court to review the decision. This brought the case before Chancellor Ray L. Brock, Jr., who was highly regarded as a jurist who possessed the intestinal fortitude to make an unpopular decision when the underlying facts demonstrated a violation of the state or federal constitutions. Chancellor Brock reversed the board's decision, holding that Cox's discharge violated his right to remain silent and ordered that Captain Cox be reinstated with full pay. Chancellor Brock's decision was ultimately upheld in an opinion by the Tennessee Court of Appeals written by Judge James Parrott and concurred in by presiding Judge Robert Cooper of Chattanooga and Judge Clifford Sanders of Kingsport.

The Tennessee Supreme Court denied the City of Chattanooga's petition for writ of certiorari in February 1974,[1] and the United States Supreme Court likewise denied the city's request for certiorari in October of that same year. The appellate decision upholding Cox's right to remain silent and thus concluding that his termination from employment violated his constitutional rights remains precedent in the state to this day.

---

1 The mechanism for seeking review in the Tennessee Supreme Court has been alternatively referred to, under rule and statute, as a petition for writ of certiorari and a petition for permission to appeal. The latter phrase is currently in use.

What I Know

1. The constitutional right at issue in both this case and the Shannon case is the privilege against self-incrimination provided for in both the federal and state constitutions.

2. The privilege against self-incrimination is found in the Fifth Amendment to the United States Constitution and in Article I, Section 99 of the Tennessee Constitution. The privilege protects an individual from being forced to give testimony that would likely incriminate him or herself. This means that an individual may not be forced to testify if the information requested would likely subject the person to a future prosecution. The privilege also applies to custodial interrogations and requires that an individual that is in custody be warned of the privilege before the individual can be interrogated by the police.

3. In this case, the captain of the fire department was fired after he, on counsel's advice, refused to talk with the Chattanooga police about a crime that occurred in Atlanta. The captain challenged his termination by bringing a civil action against the city, arguing that his firing violated his constitutional right to exercise the privilege against self-incrimination.

4. A *Miranda* warning is a concept that derives from the United States Supreme Court decision in *Miranda v. Arizona*, 384 U.S. 436 (1966). *See* Chapter 1 *supra*. In that case, the Court held that before the police may question an individual who is in custody, the individual is entitled to be advised of constitutional rights, including the right to remain silent and the right to counsel. When the individual in custody consents to speak with officers, after being informed of the rights that will be surrendered by doing so, the individual is said to have waived the *Miranda* rights.

5. An attorney may advise a client to not speak to the police out of fear that the client, either due to intimidation or manipulation, may say things that can be used against the client or that the client's statements may enable the state to build a stronger case or to question the client's honesty. An attorney may also advise a client to remain silent because the client's statement may serve as strong evidence against the client in a case under investigation or may provide other information that can be used to charge the client with a criminal offense.

Chapter V
State v. Thornton, 492 S.W.2d 912 (Tenn. 1973)

1. What is the role of the grand jury in a criminal case?

2. What is a subpoena? What does it mean to be subpoenaed to testify before a grand jury?

3. What rights are protected by the First Amendment to the United States Constitution?

4. How does the First Amendment come into play in the facts of this case?

5. What does it mean to be found in contempt of court?

6. What was the basis for finding Thornton in contempt of court?

7. What are the types of bail? What does it mean to be released on your own recognizance?

8. What does it mean to "give notice" to the opposing side?

9. Why is an attorney required to "give notice" to the opposing side?

CHAPTER V

STATE v. THORNTON
492 S.W.2d 912 (Tenn. 1973)

The opinion in *State v. Thornton*, 492 S.W.2d 912 (Tenn. 1973) does not fully convey two important behind-the-scenes dynamics. The first was the unfortunate public controversy involving Judge Charles Galbreath, a judge on the Tennessee Court of Criminal Appeals. The second was the excessive enthusiasm of a young lawyer – in this case, me – in the representation of his client. While this may seem to be two separate, unconnected stories, my representation of Thornton would lead me to Judge Galbreath and cast us both, momentarily, in the spotlight of the Tennessee Supreme Court.

First, Judge Galbreath. Judge Charles (Charlie) Galbreath was a trial lawyer who also served as a member of the Tennessee General Assembly. In 1963, Galbreath proposed the first public defender legislation that would provide for legal representation for indigent defendants in Davidson County and which, many years later, would be expanded into a state-wide public defender program. Galbreath became Davidson County's first public defender. He later would serve on the Tennessee Court of Criminal Appeals until he resigned as a result of public and political pressure for unorthodox and questionable behavior.[1]

And now to Harry Thornton. Harry Thornton was a well-known radio and television personality in southeast Tennessee and northwest Georgia. His early talk show on WDEF-TV (channel 12) had a tremendous following. He accepted calls from listeners, which he

---

1 Among the acts for which Galbreath obtained notoriety were (1) writing a letter to Larry Flynt, the editor of Hustler magazine, with sexual content, on official court stationery that included the names of all members of the Tennessee Court of Criminal Appeals; (2) buying cigars in Cuba and illegally selling them in Nashville; (3) getting arrested for "jaywalking" while intoxicated in Columbus, Ohio; and (4) performing weddings on Ferris wheels and in bars.

would often use, along with his lively and sometimes caustic person-ality, to stir up controversy and increase ratings. In addition to his media work, Thornton owned an interest in a professional wrestling venue in Tennessee.

Thornton entered the legal arena in 1972, following an on-the-air conversation with a male caller who claimed to have been a member of a recent Hamilton County Grand Jury charged with investigating whether a Chattanooga municipal judge had taken illegal gratuities from local bail bondsmen. The local prosecutor had chosen not to charge the judge, but after the investigation the judge resigned and accepted a position as a federal administrative law judge.

Thornton's caller was dissatisfied with the prosecutor's action, charging that he had engaged in a "whitewash" by failing to charge the municipal judge despite ample evidence. During the on-the-air con-versation Thornton intensified the situation by claiming that he rec-ognized the voice of the caller and that he was a good and believable man. Unfortunately, the Hamilton County District Attorney General, Edward E. Davis, was watching the show that morning and did not take kindly to the caller's characterization of his office's actions.

Thornton was subpoenaed to appear before the grand jury in November 1982. Under the auspices of investigating whether the grand juror had violated the statutory oath of secrecy imposed upon grand jurors, Thornton was asked, under oath, to identify the caller. Thornton refused, relying on his First Amendment right not to speak. Thornton was immediately cited to appear before the Honorable Till-man Grant, Judge of Division Il of the Criminal Court of Hamilton County.

Thornton came to court without a lawyer. Judge Grant advised him of his right to counsel and warned him that he could be jailed for contempt of court should he persist in refusing to identify the caller. When Thornton persisted in his refusal, Judge Grant continued the case to allow Thornton to hire a lawyer and Thornton hired me to represent him.

Given my prior experience as an assistant district attorney serv-ing in Judge Grant's courtroom, and my client's adamant refusal to re-veal the identity of the caller, I quickly realized that there was a strong potential that he would go to jail. To prepare for this inevitability, I decided to prepare to appeal and to secure bond for my client during the appeal. Enter Judge Galbreath. I contacted the appellate judge for those purposes, but unfortunately and incorrectly, I did not give the State of Tennessee notice of my intentions or my actions. To my surprise, Judge Galbreath told me to draft a proposed order and he would release Thornton "on his own recognizance," meaning that Thornton would not have to post money to be released pending appeal.

Continuing to zealously represent my client, and without giving further thought to my need to comply with the customary and ethical requirement of giving my adversary notice of filing, I employed Gary Gerbitz, who had served as a former assistant district attorney (and would later be elected as Hamilton County District Attorney). Gerbitz would travel to Nashville on the date of my client's hearing and wait in Judge Galbreath's office for my call. In the event my prediction was correct, Gerbitz would present a petition for bail and a proposed order releasing my client on his own recognizance for Judge Galbreath's signature.

As expected, my client remained steadfast in his refusal to identify the mystery caller and Judge Grant found him guilty of contempt of court and ordered him incarcerated until he revealed the name of the alleged grand juror. As he was walked to the Hamilton County Jail before the television cameras and reporters, Thornton proudly adhered to his First Amendment rights as a reporter and newsperson. Meanwhile, my colleague secured Judge Galbreath's signature on the proposed order releasing Thornton on his own recognizance and made a quick return to Chattanooga, where we filed the order with the Criminal Court Clerk's office, resulting in Thornton's release from custody within three hours.

Obviously, this quick action did not sit well with either the local district attorney, state Attorney General's office, or the criminal court judge (although he remained silent). I pursued a series of unsuccessful proceedings, while the prosecution pursued an appeal of Judge Galbreath's order to the Tennessee Supreme Court. Candidly, at this point I was becoming concerned not only about my client's incarceration, but also about my own, as well as about the future of my law license in the State of Tennessee. In a futile effort to cleanse myself of any wrongdoing I filed a motion to set bond in Judge Grant's court.

The State's appeal was granted on December 15, 1972, Justice Chattin set bail in the amount of $1,000, and the case was set for oral argument on January 11, 1973. During oral argument, the Honorable Hayes Cooney of the Tennessee Attorney General's Office and Justice Chattin did a good job of raking me over the proverbial coals for not giving my opponent proper notice and for not exercising the proper procedure for appealing Thornton's case. When I stood up to present my argument defending my client and Judge Galbreath's actions, it would be a great understatement to say that I was extremely apologetic for the actions I had pursued in defense of my client. During Justice Chattin's harsh reprimand, I was gravely concerned about the future of my client, Judge Galbreath, and myself.

Despite the scolding, what happened next is one of those memorable experiences that, despite my more than fifty years as a lawyer, I will never forget. As I continued to apologize, Justice Allison Humphreys came to my rescue in a manner that became permanently embedded in my mind. Justice Humphreys interrupted my argument and stated, "Young man you don't have to apologize for anything that you did to protect the interests of your client. And, by the way, if I ever need a lawyer to defend me, you are the one I am going to call."

The court's brief opinion, authored by Special Justice John W. Wilson, declared "that the order Judge Galbreath, made on December 5, 1972, is void." *State v. Thornton*, 492 S.W.2d at 915. The contempt case against Thornton lay idle and ultimately would be dismissed without further publicity. Judge Galbreath would resign from the appellate court under strong political and judicial pressure in 1978; Harry Thornton would continue to receive high ratings for his controversial talk show on Channel 12 until 1992; and I would never again, in my now fifty-six years of practice, fail to give proper notice to opposing counsel.

What I Know

1. The grand jury's role is to hear the prosecutor's evidence against an accused to determine if probable cause exists to believe that a crime was committed and the accused committed it. If the grand jury finds that probable cause exists, the grand jury issues a document charging the accused with the appropriate crime or crimes. This document is known as an indictment or "true bill." If the grand jury does not find probable cause, then they will issue a "no true bill." All grand jury proceedings are held in secret.

2. A subpoena is a directive ordering an individual to appear in court, at a deposition, or at a hearing. When an individual receives a subpoena to testify before the grand jury, the person is required to appear before the grand jury, be sworn, and answer any questions posed by the prosecution or grand jurors. Sometimes individuals subpoenaed before the grand jury will seek advice of counsel and, relying on that advice, will invoke the right to remain silent, refusing to testify before the grand jury for fear that their testimony might tend to incriminate them.

3. The First Amendment to the United States Constitution protects the freedoms of: (1) speech, (2) press, (3) religion, (4) assembly, and (5) petition.

4. The First Amendment came into play in this case because Thornton was a reporter who refused to identify the source who informed Thornton about an investigation of a judge, allegedly bribed by bail bondsmen. Thornton, as a member of the press, was exercising his First Amendment right not to speak. Most journalists take the position that they are protected both by the First Amendment and by privilege laws from revealing their sources because the press plays an essential role as a "neutral watchdog" and protector of democracy.

5. To be found "in contempt of court" means that a person has disrespected the court in some way, either through in-court behavior or by deliberately disobeying the orders of the court.

6. In this case, Thornton was found in contempt of court for refusing to answer the court's questions as to the identity of the grand juror who had called his talk show. Thornton was cited to court when he initially refused to answer the same question in the grand jury.

7. The posting of bail is for the purpose of securing an individual's later appearance at court. Bail may be posted in cash or by means of security either in the form of a property bond or a bond insured by a bail bond company. Accused may also be released on personal recognizance, known as PR or ROR (released on recognizance), which means that the accused promises to return to court and is released from detention without posting payment or security.

8. To "give notice" to the opposing side means to inform them of the action you are taking. Attorneys give notice by serving a copy of all documents filed in a case upon the opposing counsel or on an unrepresented party.

9. An attorney is required to give notice in order to give the opposing side an opportunity to respond and state their position on the matter before the court takes action.

Chapter VI
McKeldin v. State, 516 S.W.2d 82 (Tenn. 1974)

1.   How do the decisions of the United States Supreme Court affect the operation of state courts?

2.   How do the decisions of other federal courts affect the operation of state courts?

3.   May a state provide greater liberties to its citizens than those provided by the United States Constitution as interpreted by the United States Supreme Court?

4.   What is a "critical stage" of a prosecution?

5.   Why does the right to counsel only apply to critical stages of a prosecution?

6.   What is the purpose of a preliminary hearing in a criminal case?

7.   Why is a preliminary hearing a "critical stage" of a prosecution?

8.   What is prejudicial error?

9.   What is harmless error?

10. How can a violation of the United States Constitution be harmless error?

CHAPTER VI

McKELDIN v. STATE
516 S.W.2d 82 (Tenn. 1974)

Darryl Lamont McKeldin was arrested on August 1, 1972, and charged with armed robbery. Because McKeldin was indigent,[1] the Chattanooga city judge appointed an individual by the name of Isiah Ewing to represent McKeldin at his preliminary hearing.

Ewing was not an attorney, but had been mistaken for one when he previously appeared as a witness, nicely dressed in a coat and tie. The city judge erroneously thought Ewing was an attorney and asked if he had any questions for the witnesses. Although Ewing did not ask any questions, he was impressed that the judicial officer had mistaken him for an attorney, so he began impersonating one.

Ewing opened an office with an attorney, Mickey Cash, and rented another small office near the city court. With the help of the city judges, a few friendly bail bonding companies, and some police officers, Ewing soon developed a thriving law practice. Ewing applied to become a member of the Chattanooga Bar Association, asserting that he was a graduate of Vanderbilt Law School. When a search of the list of alumni from the prestigious university and the roster of licensed attorneys in Tennessee revealed no "Isiah Ewing," Ewing was revealed to be an impostor, with no authority to practice law or represent clients.[2]

But that discovery was a few weeks after Ewing had "represented" McKeldin at his preliminary hearing. Once Ewing's ruse had been discovered, McKeldin hired me as his counsel, and we filed a mo-

---

1 "Indigent" comes from the Latin word for "wanting," and indicates a condition of being without, as in lacking resources to afford to hire counsel.
2 In the collateral chancery court proceedings, on September 12, 1975, Hamilton County Chancellor Herschel P. Franks held self-appointed lawyer Ewing in contempt of court, enjoined him from engaging in the practice of law, and sentenced him to serve ten days in the Silverdale Workhouse.

tion to dismiss the charges on the basis that McKeldin was denied his right, under the Sixth Amendment of the United States Constitution, to effective assistance of counsel at the preliminary hearing, "a critical stage of a criminal proceeding" because Isiah Ewing was not duly qualified as an attorney. In the alternative we requested that the case be remanded to city court for a preliminary hearing. The motion, and several other motions to quash the indictment, were overruled and the defendant was convicted and sentenced to twenty years in the state penitentiary. After conviction, our appeal to the Tennessee Court of Criminal Appeals was also unsuccessful.

Convinced that our client had been denied his constitutional right to counsel at a preliminary stage in the proceeding, we asked the Tennessee Supreme Court to grant an appeal on that and six other issues. The state supreme court, in an opinion authored by Justice Joe Henry, followed the precedent of the United States Supreme Court in *Coleman v. Alabama*, 399 U.S. 1 (1970) and held that because a preliminary hearing in Tennessee is a critical stage in a criminal proceeding, the accused has a constitutional right to be represented by counsel. *McKeldin v. State*, 516 S.W.2d 82, 86 (Tenn. 1974).

In reaching this decision, Justice Henry was required to confront a decision by the federal appeals court that reached the opposite result. In *Harris v. Neil*, 437 F.2d 63 (6th Cir. 1971), the United States Court of Appeals for the Sixth Circuit had held that there was no constitutional right to a preliminary hearing, that a preliminary hearing was not a critical stage of the prosecution in Tennessee, and, therefore, the accused did not have a right to counsel at a preliminary hearing. But as Justice Henry noted, the *Harris* decision was issued before the Tennessee General Assembly adopted a statute, providing:

> In all criminal cases, prior to presentment and indictment, whether the charge be a misdemeanor or a felony, the accused shall be entitled to a preliminary hearing upon his request therefore, whether the grand jury of the county be in session or not.

Tenn. Code Ann. §40-1131(1971). On the other hand, McKeldin's preliminary hearing occurred after the effective date of the statute. Based on the statutory right to a preliminary hearing, Justice Henry concluded that, in Tennessee, a preliminary hearing was a critical stage of the prosecution because it was the type of proceeding at which "certain rights may be sacrificed or lost." *McKeldin v. State,* 516 S.W.2d at 85.

Next, Justice Henry turned to the issue of the right to counsel. Reverting back to his experience as a criminal defense lawyer, Justice Henry, perhaps unexpectedly described the role of counsel in a manner that would lead the Tennessee's Attorney General and law enforcement agencies to band together to attempt to amend – and eventually succeed in amending – the statute in an effort to diminish the value of the preliminary hearing as a defense discovery tool. Justice Henry noted that

> Every criminal lawyer "worth his salt" knows the overriding importance and the manifest advantages of a preliminary hearing. In fact the failure to exploit this golden opportunity to observe the manner, demeanor and appearance of the witnesses for the prosecution, to learn the precise details of the prosecution's case, and to engage in that happy event sometimes known as a "fishing expedition," would be an inexcusable dereliction of duty in the majority of cases.[3]

Id. at 85-86.

A unanimous Tennessee Supreme Court reversed McKeldin's conviction, holding that he had been denied his constitutional rights. But, the justices remanded his case to determine whether McKeldin

---

3 When the Tennessee Rules of Criminal Procedure were adopted, the Advisory Commission on the Rules of Practice and Procedure had only a single criminal defense member in its number. In addressing Justice Henry's language in McKeldin, the Advisory Commission noted that

> [d]espite the language in McKeldin v. State, 516 SW.2d 82 (Tenn. 1974) suggesting that this stage of the proceeding is a discovery procedure for the accused, it is the commission's position, to the contrary, that McKeldin [sic] does not convert the preliminary hearing into a "fishing expedition," with unlimited potential for discovery. The case holds that the preliminary hearing is a probable cause hearing, which can result in providing discovery to the defendant, an important byproduct of its probable cause function.

Advisory Commission Comments, Tenn. R. Crim. P. 5.1.

"was prejudiced by this denial of a constitutionally guaranteed right" or whether the constitutional error was "harmless." [4]

On April 22, 1975, after several days of hearings, Criminal Court Judge Joe DiRisio held that McKeldin had not been prejudiced by the fact that the non-lawyer, Ewing, had represented him at his preliminary hearing and reinstated McKeldin's twenty-year armed robbery conviction. The Tennessee Court of Criminal Appeals affirmed later that year, and the Tennessee Supreme Court denied a writ of certiorari on the issue. Judge DiRisio ordered that the State of Tennessee pay me four hundred dollars ($400) for my representation of McKeldin in the remand proceedings.

---

4 In *Chapman v. California*, 386 U.S. 18 (1967), the United States Supreme Court explained that unless "there is a reasonable probability that the (error) complained of might have contributed to the conviction," the error is harmless and does not justify relief on appeal. *386 U.S. at 24* (quoting *Fahy v. Connecticut*, 375 U.S. 85, 86-87 (1963))

What I Know

1.   A United States Supreme Court decision that interprets federal constitutional rights that are applicable to the states is binding on state courts. In this case, the Supreme Court precedent in *Coleman v. Alabama*, applied both federal constitutional law (the Sixth Amendment right to counsel) and Alabama state law.

2.   The decisions of federal district (trial) and appellate courts interpreting federal statutes are not binding on state courts. Decisions of the federal courts that interpret provisions of the United States Constitution are applicable in state courts, when the particular federal constitutional provision has been interpreted to apply to the states. Often, a federal court will be required to apply state law. For example, the federal appeals decision referenced here, *Harris v. Neil*, initially interpreted Tennessee law, but the Tennessee law had changed by the time the case got to the Tennessee Supreme Court.

3.   A state may provide its citizens with greater liberties than the United States Constitution requires; in effect, the United States Constitution provides the floor beneath which the state cannot go.

4.   A "critical stage" of a prosecution is one in which the "guiding hand of counsel" might help assure the fair trial rights of the accused. In this case, the issue was whether a preliminary hearing is a critical stage of the prosecution. The Tennessee Supreme Court ruled that a preliminary hearing is a critical stage of a prosecution.

5.   The right to counsel applies to critical stages of a prosecution, because it is in those circumstances that the right to counsel is most necessary to assuring fairness. In parts of the prosecution that are not adversarial, such as grand jury proceedings, the right to counsel does not apply.

6.   The purpose of a preliminary hearing is to allow a neutral judge to determine whether the state has sufficient evidence to establish that probable cause exists to believe that the charged crime occurred and the defendant committed it. The role of the judge is to test the prosecution's case to make sure that the evidence is sufficient for the case to move forward and, conversely, to release the defendant if the proof is insufficient to establish probable cause. If the judge finds probable cause, the case is "bound over" to the grand jury, which also conducts a probable cause determination.

7.   A preliminary hearing is a critical stage of a prosecution because at this stage, the accused gains some insight as to the nature and strength of the prosecution's case against the accused. It also gives the accused the opportunity to hear the witness' testimony, observe their demeanor, and cross-examine.

8.   Prejudicial error refers to an error that undermines the reliability of the verdict. When a trial court makes a prejudicial error, an appellate court will take steps to correct the error, which may include granting the accused a new trial and, in rare circumstances, dismissing the case.

9.   Harmless error refers to an error that does not undermine the reliability of the verdict. When a trial court makes an error that is harmless, the appellate court will point out the error but will not grant any relief to the accused.

10. A constitutional violation may be considered harmless error because some other process or procedure substituted for or cured the earlier violation. For example, if a defendant's preliminary hearing rights are violated, but the defendant later gets convicted at trial or pleads guilty, any doubts regarding probable cause have been resolved either at trial, when the prosecution established the defendant's guilt beyond a reasonable doubt, or when the defendant admitted guilt to the charged offense.

Chapter VII
Day & Zimmerman, Inc. v. Challoner, 423 U.S. 3 (1975)

1. What does "jurisdiction" mean?

2. What does "conflict of laws" mean?

3. What does "choice of law" mean?

4. May a lawyer represent clients and appear in courts in states in which the lawyer is not licensed to practice?

5. What is meant by the professional requirement that a lawyer provide "competent" representation?

6. How does a lawyer acquire sufficient knowledge to handle complex cases?

CHAPTER VII

DAY & ZIMMERMAN, INC. v. CHALLONER
423 U.S. 3 (1975) (per curiam)

I tried this civil products liability case along with the late Cahill Hitt, a Texas attorney. Product liability cases are based on the doctrine of strict liability. That doctrine imposes responsibility on those who design, manufacture, distribute, or sell faulty or dangerous products that, ultimately, injure users.

Two soldiers, David Nelms of Tennessee and Harley Challoner of Wisconsin, were serving in the United States Army in Cambodia in May, 1970, where the United States was engaged in combat with the North Vietnamese. Helms was killed and Challoner was seriously injured when a 105 Howitzer[1] prematurely detonated and backfired, causing an explosion. According to members of the gun crew and several experts, all applicable safety procedures were followed during the firing of the artillery. The explosion was caused by a cavitation in the explosive material that had been poured into the artillery shells by the manufacturer.[2]

Co-counsel and I filed the case in the United States District Court for the Eastern District of Texas, located in Texarkana, Texas, based on "diversity jurisdiction." Diversity jurisdiction gives the federal court the authority to hear a case when the parties are citizens of different states in the United States. The 105 Howitzer at issue was manufactured by Day & Zimmerman, Inc., a company that was incorporated in Maryland but had its principal place of business in Pennsylvania. The particular howitzer at issue was made in a factory in Texarkana, Texas, while component parts were made in Milan,

---

1 According to Merriam- Webster's Dictionary, a howitzer is a "short cannon used to fire projectiles at medium muzzle velocities and with relatively high trajectories." The 105 Howitzer was developed and used by the United States.

2 A cavitation occurs when gas bubbles are formed in a liquid due to changes in the liquid's pressure.

Tennessee, and other locations. The injured soldiers were citizens of Tennessee and Wisconsin respectively. Thus, because of the diversity of citizenship between all the parties, the federal district court had jurisdiction to hear the products liability action.

The question that remained for the federal court was the question of "choice of law." In other words, which jurisdiction's law determined what substantive product liability law applied in the case? Ultimately the answer to that question would determine whether the law of Maryland, Pennsylvania, Tennessee, or Wisconsin, where the parties resided; the law of Texas, where the product was manufactured; or the law of Cambodia, where the product exploded and caused injury and death, applied.

In diversity cases, the general rule was that the choice of law rules of the forum state, i.e., the state where the case was filed, would be applied to determine which state's substantive law applied. *Erie v. Tompkins*, 304 U.S. 64 (1938); *Klaxon v. Stentor Electric Manufacturing Company, Inc.*, 313 U.S. 487 (1941). Using the general rule, the Texas choice of law provisions would be used to determine which state's products liability law applied. Under Texas law, the governing substantive law was the law of the place where the injury occurred. But because Cambodia had no interest whatsoever in the case, the trial court applied the Texas substantive product liability law and, based on that law, the jury imposed liability on the manufacturer and, ultimately, awarded two hundred thousand dollars ($200,000) to Challoner and forty thousand ($40,000) to the administrator of Nelms' estate.

The manufacturer appealed arguing that the trial court should have applied the strict liability law of Cambodia.[3] Co-counsel Hitt successfully handled the appeal in the United States Court of Appeals for the Fifth Circuit, which affirmed the district court noting that the general rule relied upon by the manufacturer "does not extend so far as to bind a federal court to the law of a wholly disinterested jurisdiction." *Challoner v. Day & Zimmerman*, Inc., 512 F.2d 77, 81 (5th Cir.), *reh. denied*, (1975).

---

3 Research revealed that the strict liability law of Cambodia applied only to "chickens and goats" and therefore was not applicable in product liability cases.

When the manufacturer sought certiorari in the United States Supreme Court, Hitt filed the responsive brief on behalf of our clients. The Supreme Court, in a per curiam opinion, agreed with the manufacturer's argument, and held that federal courts were bound to follow the state choice of law rules in diversity actions. *Davis & Zimmerman v. Challoner*, 423 U.S. 3, 5 (1975). The case was remanded to the appeals court to "identify and follow the Texas conflicts rule." *Id.* The case was subsequently settled between the parties following a remand to the trial court and after adding pretrial and post-trial interest.

This case demonstrates how complex law can be and how important it is for lawyers to be competent in all areas in which they practice.[4] Not only did we have to become knowledgeable about the manufacturing of artillery shells and potential causes of unanticipated explosions, we also had to research the procedural and substantive law of multiple states and a foreign jurisdiction.

---

4 The importance of acquiring professional competence is often downplayed by lawyers who solicit cases through generalized advertisements.

What I Know

1. As used in the phrase "diversity jurisdiction," the word "jurisdiction" refers to a court's ability to hear and adjudicate a case as provided either by state or federal constitutions or law.

2. The "conflict of laws" principle refers to the rules that courts use to determine which state's law applies to a case when the parties or issues may be governed by laws in different states. When various laws may apply, the court that is hearing the case (the forum court) must first decide which jurisdiction's law must be used to decide the case. In this case, because the parties were residents of three different states, the product was manufactured in a fourth state, and the injury occurred in a foreign country, the first issue that had to be resolved was which jurisdiction's law applied.3. Each state has "choice of law" provisions, by statute or judicial decision, that dictate which law applies when cases are filed in courts in the state. In contracts, the parties often choose which law that will apply if a dispute arises in a provision known as a "choice of laws" provision. In this case, because there was a conflict of laws issue, the choice of law provisions of Texas, the forum state, determined which jurisdiction's law would apply.

4. An attorney may not practice law in a state in which the attorney is not licensed. Many states allow for pro hac vice admission, which allows an attorney who is not licensed in that jurisdiction to practice law with the court's permission in particular matters.

5. Competent representation requires the legal knowledge, skill, thoroughness, and preparation reasonably necessary for the representation. It depends on several factors, such as the complexity of the case, the lawyer's level of experience in this and similar types of cases, and the lawyer's ability to become sufficiently knowledgeable about

the subject matter, along with a number of other factors.

6. A lawyer can acquire competence in a complex matter by undertaking a thorough legal and factual investigation, researching and studying the subject matter, and, if appropriate, associating experienced counsel or consulting experts to collaborate on the case.

Chapter VIII
Graham v. State, 547 S.W.2d 531 (1977)

1. Because no law provided for state-funded psychiatric examinations for defendants, what was the likely basis for court-appointed counsel's request?

2. What does "criminal responsibility" mean?

3. How does an accused's mental health impact responsibility for criminal conduct?

4. What is an amicus curiae? What is an amicus curiae brief?

5. What does it mean for a case to be pending?

CHAPTER VIII

GRAHAM v. STATE
547 S.W.2d 531 (Tenn.), reh. denied, (Tenn. 1977)

The Sixth Amendment provides a right to counsel for the "accused." The right applies regardless of the accused's ability to afford counsel. Thus, if a person is unable to afford counsel, the State provides counsel either through appointment or by means of a state-wide contract or public defender system. Prior to Tennessee's adoption of a state-wide public defender system, courts appointed private attorneys to represent indigent defendants. The appointment system gave younger lawyers an opportunity to gain experience, but even more experienced lawyers, who did not normally practice criminal law, were sometimes appointed.

Such was the case in the *State of Tennessee v. Larry Gene Graham.* 547 S.W.2d 531 (Tenn. 1977). Judge Campbell Carden appointed his friend, Thomas A. Harris, a respected member of the Chattanooga Bar who normally defended insurance companies in civil cases, primarily involving automobile accidents. Despite his lack of experience in criminal defense, attorney Harris' work in Graham's case provides a noteworthy example of an excellent civil lawyer providing exceptional representation for an accused in a serious criminal case.

Graham was charged with bank robbery, grand larceny, and assault with intent to commit murder. Realizing the seriousness of the charges and learning that his client had a history of treatment in psychiatric hospitals, Tom Harris tried to get the court to appoint a psychiatrist to examine Graham. The trial court refused the request, finding no legal basis for a state-appointed psychiatrist. Relying solely on a defense of insanity, Graham testified, admitted each offense, and was convicted on all charges. The Tennessee Court of Criminal Appeals affirmed the conviction.

Attorney Harris pursued an appeal to the Tennessee Supreme Court, encouraging the court to find that his client had been denied his right to a state-funded psychiatric examination and to introduce medical records from his prior psychiatric hospitalizations. Although the state supreme court did not recognize a right to a state-appointed psychiatrist,[1] the court agreed that the defendant's medical records from mental health facilities should have been allowed in evidence.[2] Additionally, the court took the opportunity to evaluate the various tests for determining criminal responsibility. Because of the significance and the potential ramifications of this issue, attorney Harris requested assistance from the Tennessee Association of Criminal Defense Lawyers (TACDL). When the Amicus Curiae Committee of TACDL approved the filing of an amicus brief on behalf of TACDL, I was chosen to draft the brief.

Before the Tennessee Supreme Court, we divided the oral argument time. Attorney Harris addressed the business records issue, and I urged the court to abandon the *M'Naghten* rules that were being used to determine criminal responsibility.[3] As it happened, both of us were successful and Graham's convictions were overturned. In addition to finding that the trial judge should have admitted Graham's medical records, the Tennessee Supreme Court decisively rejected the

---

1 Good lawyers think beyond the existing law, urging courts to grant their clients' rights and protections that have not yet been recognized but are rooted in fundamental fairness and equal justice under the law. In this case, for example, counsel urged the court to give an indigent defendant a right to a state-furnished expert who could assist in developing Graham's insanity defense, which required the defense to show that Graham suffered from a defect of reason because of a disease of the mind. Although counsel lost his argument in *Graham*, the United States Supreme Court would recognize the right of indigent defendants to court-appointed experts less than ten years later. *Ake v. Oklahoma*, 470 U.S. 68 (1985) (holding that due process requires that the State provide a psychiatrist's assistance to an indigent defendant who has made a preliminary showing that sanity at the time of the offense is likely to be an important issue in the case).

2 As a civil trial lawyer, Tom Harris was well experienced in admitting business records under Tennessee law, the Uniform Business Records as Evidence Act, codified at the time as Tenn. Code Ann. §§24-712-715.

3 The so-called *M'Naghten* rules derive from *M'Naghten's* Case, 1 C. & K. 130, 10 CL. & F. 200, 8 Eng. Rep. 718, which was decided by the House of Lords in 1843. Under the rules, to avoid criminal responsibility on the grounds of insanity, an individual must be suffering such a "defect of reason, from disease of the mind, as not to know the nature and quality of the act he was doing; or, if he did know it that he did not know what he was doing was wrong." 8 Eng. Rep. at 722.

M'Naghten rules, replacing the rules with the test set out in the Model Penal Code.[4]

> We think that unquestionably the [*M'Naghten*] rules tend to enforce outmoded and erroneous psychological theories, tend to limit or distort psychiatric testimony, focus on the ability to distinguish between right and wrong, ignoring the individual's ability to exercise self-control; focus on cognition and ignore the volitional aspects of personality; and punish persons for conduct beyond their capacity of control. In a word, [the] application is an impediment to the fair trial that is a part of the birthright of every American citizen.

Graham v. State, 547 S.W.2d at 540.

The Tennessee Supreme Court's adoption of a new test for determining criminal responsibility did not trigger a reversal of Graham's case, but the exclusion of his medical records did. After Graham's convictions were reversed, Tom Harris urged the trial judge and the prosecution to send Graham to a mental hospital because of his complicated history of mental illness. The court was eventually persuaded and Graham was sent to the Middle Tennessee Mental Health Hospital. To everyone's dismay, Graham was released after being hospitalized for only six weeks.

Although the new criminal responsibility test did not benefit Graham directly, it was critically important to others, including my client Leonard Griffey, whose case, discussed in Chapter IX, was pending in the Tennessee Court of Criminal Appeals at the time the Supreme Court abandoned the *M'Naghten* rules. This experience demonstrates the necessity of staying abreast of "pipeline cases," cases that are in the appellate courts awaiting review or pending decision.

---

4 Section 4.01 of the Model Penal Code provided that criminal responsibility was lacking when, as a result of mental disease or defect, a person lacked "substantial capacity either to appreciate the wrongfulness of his conduct or to conform his conduct to the requirements of law." *Graham v. State*, 547 S.W. 2d at 543 (noting that the court replaced the word "criminality" with the word "wrongfulness" in the definition it adopted).

Justice Joe Henry, who authored the *Graham* opinion would continue to strive to assure fairness for defendants who suffered from mental illness. A few years after *Graham*, in a dissenting opinion, Justice Henry observed that:

> Those knowledgeable in the field of criminal law recognize that the defense of insanity is scorned by prosecuting attorneys, abused by some defense lawyers, viewed with distrust by juries, scrutinized with suspicion by many trial judges and tends to fall apart on the appellate level. And yet all concerned must recognize that a person who is truly insane is entitled to fair treatment in a court of law.

State v. Stacy, 601 S.W. 2d 696, 706 (Tenn. 1980) (Henry, J., dissenting).

What I Know

1. Although at the time of this case, no state law provided for state-funded psychiatric evaluations, counsel raised the issue based on his duty to represent his client competently and zealously and in light of his awareness of his client's mental condition. Under the law, an individual must both be competent to stand trial and must have had the mental capacity to be criminally responsible at the time of the crime. To be competent to stand trial, an accused must be able to understand and assist in the proceedings. Here, counsel was likely concerned about both his client's competence and his client's capacity to be criminally responsible. Additionally, counsel undoubtedly raised the issue because of his client's right to fundamental fairness and due process of law. In this circumstance, counsel reasoned that due process of law should provide the same access to psychiatric evaluations for an indigent accused as a non-indigent accused would have.

2. "Criminal responsibility" refers to whether an individual who has been charged with committing a crime has the requisite mental state (mens rea) to enable him to be held accountable and punished for committing that crime.

3. Fundamental principles of criminal law dictate that to be punished for criminal conduct, a person must both engage in criminal act or conduct (actus reus) and have the necessary mental intent (mens rea) to commit the crime. An accused's mental health can impact responsibility for criminal conduct by absolving the accused of criminal conduct if their mental status was impaired such that they could not appreciate what they were doing or appreciate that the conduct was wrong. In such a case, mens rea would be absent and the accused may be adjudged not guilty by reason of insanity or, in some jurisdictions, guilty but insane.

4. The phrase "amicus curiae" means "friend of the court." An amicus curiae is a brief filed (commonly in the United States Supreme Court or a state's highest court by those interested in, but not parties to, a case, urging a particular ruling. Often, amicus briefs will be filed by organizations that have an interest in the outcome of a case. Here, for example, the association of criminal defense lawyers in the state filed a brief to urge to court to reconsider the state's definition of insanity as it related to criminal responsibility.

5. When a case is pending, that means that it is not yet decided. These cases are sometimes referred to as "pipeline cases." It is important to remain aware of pending cases because the ruling may be advantageous to a position you wish to take in a case.

Chapter IX
State v. Griffey

1. How do the *M'Naghten* and Model Penal Code tests for insanity as it relates to criminal responsibility differ? How does the test a state applies make a difference in an individual case?

2. What does it mean to be held without bond?

3. In this case, what was the purpose of having medical experts testify?

4. What does it mean to submit a special jury instruction?

5. What is a motion for a new trial? When is it filed? What is its purpose?

CHAPTER IX

STATE v. GRIFFEY[1]

My involvement as amicus in *Graham v. State*, 547 S.W.2d 531 (Tenn. 1977) aided my representation of Leonard Griffey, whose case was pending at around the same time. Leonard Griffey was accused of murdering his estranged wife and her young boss, her alleged lover, in Red Bank, Tennessee. The State charged Leonard with two counts of first-degree murder and sought the death penalty. The State of Tennessee was aggressively represented by the late John Goza who had left his former employer, Tennessee Valley Authority, to become a prosecutor.

Leonard Griffey was held without bond and would not secure freedom for more than five years. Recognizing the severity of the offense and the lack of any evidence to support self-defense, I requested that my client undergo a psychiatric examination at the Middle Tennessee Psychiatric Hospital in Murfreesboro to determine whether he was competent to stand trial and whether he met the standard for criminal responsibility under the current *M'Naghten* rules in effect in Tennessee.[2]

At trial, both the prosecution and the defense called medical experts to testify. The medical experts had different opinions regarding whether Leonard Griffey was not guilty by reason of insanity under the *M'Naghen* test. Additionally, we offered evidence to try to mitigate the seriousness of the offense and possibly justify a finding of insanity, based on Leonard's belief that his wife was having an affair with a much younger and more handsome man. My efforts to convince the jury to find Leonard guilty of a lesser homicide offense were un-

---

1 Neither Westlaw, nor Lexis, nor the Tennessee Supreme Court webpage includes any digital copy of any order or opinion in this case.
2 See Chapter VIII, note 3 *supra*.

successful as Prosecutor Goza pressed hard for first-degree murder convictions and a death sentence.

At the last minute, I decided to raise an issue that might help on appeal, should Leonard be convicted. I objected to the application of the *M'Naghten* rules and submitted a special jury instruction based on the American Law Institute Model Penal Code (MPC) test on insanity which provided:

> (1) A person is not responsible for criminal conduct if at the time of such conduct as a result of mental disease or defect he lacks substantial capacity either to appreciate the criminality of his conduct or to conform his conduct to the requirements of the law.
>
> (2) As used ..., the terms "mental disease or defect" do not include any abnormality manifested only by repeated criminal or otherwise antisocial conduct.

Graham v. State, 547 S.W.2d at 543 (quoting Section 4.01 of the 1962 version of the Model Penal Code).

The MPC standard for finding a lack of criminal responsibility based on insanity was more inclusive than that set out in the predecessor *M'Naghten* rules. Under the MPC standard, a person was not responsible for criminal conduct if at the time of the conduct, as a result of "mental disease or defect," the person lacks the "substantial capacity" to *either* (1) appreciate the criminality of his conduct *or* to (2) confirm the conduct to the requirements of the law.

Based on his general practice of following precedent, Judge Campbell Carden, of the Hamilton County Criminal Court, refused to grant my request for a special jury instruction based on the MPC. Ironically, in light of the overwhelming evidence against Griffey, I was concerned that Judge Carden might act cautiously and issue the instruction. Had he given the special jury instruction as requested, my appellate issue likely would have vanished.

Not unexpectedly, Griffey was convicted of two counts of first-degree murder and was sentenced to death. I timely filed a motion for new trial, which Judge Carden overruled and a notice of appeal to the Tennessee Court of Criminal Appeals at Knoxville.

Leonard Griffey would remain incarcerated at the Hamilton County Jail during his appeal. Because Leonard was a well-behaved prisoner, he became a trustee, and developed the respect and friendship of the jail officers. These relationships would serve Leonard well when he received a new trial.

During the time that Leonard's appeal was moving through the appellate court system, as noted, I was drafting an amicus curiae brief on behalf of the Tennessee Association of Criminal Defense Lawyers (TACDL) in a separate case, *State v. Graham*, 547 S.W.2d 531 (Tenn. 1977), in which attorney Tom Harris was likewise asking the Tennessee Supreme Court to modify the *M'Naghten* rules and adopt a less restrictive test for insanity. *See* Chapter VIII, *supra*.

While Leonard's case was pending on appeal, we were successful in Graham's case, and the Tennessee Supreme Court, in an opinion authored by Justice Joe Henry, abandoned the *M'Naghten* rules in favor of the MPC test, holding:

> The Model Penal Code standards[3] will be applied (1) in all criminal trials or retrials beginning on or after the date of the release of this opinion and (2) *in all cases wherein appropriate special requests were submitted during the trial of the action*, or the issue otherwise was fairly raised in the trial court and supported by competent and credible testimony, and the conviction has not become final. Under no set of circumstances will the rule be applied to the advantage of any defendant whose conviction has already become final, i.e., where appellate review through the courts of this state has been completed.

State v. Graham, 547 S.W.2d at 543 (emphasis added).

Because of the court's careful delineation of when the standard would apply, Graham did not receive the benefit of the new test, but Leonard Griffey did. Ironically, since I had requested the special jury instruction during Griffey's trial, his was the only case in the State of

---

3 *See* note 4, Chapter VIII, *supra*, explaining that Justice Henry replaced the word "criminality" with "wrongfulness" in Tennessee's version of the MPC. *Graham v. State*, 547 S.W.2d at 543.

Tennessee that was reversed and he was the only defendant to receive a new trial due to the decision in *Graham*. Leonard Griffey's convictions were set aside very quietly and his case remanded back to Judge Carden by a simple order.

By the time of his re-trial, Leonard Griffey had been in custody for more than five years. Armed with the new MPC insanity standard[4] and the testimony of our expert witnesses, our proof was more persuasive at the second trial. Possibly, the most compelling evidence offered on Leonard's behalf was the testimony of the jailers and correctional officers who had observed and worked with Leonard during his incarceration. They testified that Leonard was not a violent person by nature and that the shooting had occurred because Leonard held a sincere belief that his wife and her younger boss were engaged in a liaison when Leonard found them at his apartment in the early morning on the day of the shooting.

This time, the jury returned a verdict of not guilty by reason of insanity, and Leonard was sentenced to a state psychiatric hospital in order to receive treatment for his mental illness. It is my best recollection that Leonard served less than six additional months before being released.

When I proposed the jury instruction on the MPC insanity standard, I was following a practice I adopted early in my career of always trying to make a record and preserve issues that could be raised on appeal. Whether as a result of that practice, or because of blind luck, my last-minute action of filing the proposed jury instruction in Leonard Griffey's case literally saved his life; indeed, that routine practice has saved many clients.

---

4 The MPC standard instruction would remain in effect until 1995 when the Tennessee General Assembly, under pressure from prosecutors, substantially modified the standard for insanity for crimes committed on or after July 1, 1995. The new law, Tenn. Code Ann. §39-11-501(a) provides that "it is an affirmative defense to a prosecution that, at the time of the commission of the acts constituting the offense, the defendant, as a result of a severe mental disease or defect, was unable to appreciate the nature or wrongfulness of the defendant's acts. Mental disease or defect does not otherwise constitute a defense. The defendant has the burden of proving the defense of insanity by clear and convincing evidence." This statute is patterned after the similar federal statute contained in 18 U.S.C. § 517.

Leonard Griffey's case offers a cautionary tale about why lawyers must remain aware of issues that are raised in cases that are pending on appeal and raise those issues in their own cases. Only by raising the issue at the trial court will the lawyer be able to use favorable case law to the client's advantage on appeal.

What I Know

1. As the author states, the Model Penal Code test is broader than the *M'Naghten* test. The word "substantial" in the Model Penal Code test makes it much easier to establish a defense based on insanity. The test a state uses can make a substantial difference in individual cases, especially in cases like this, in which whether the defendant meets the standard is a close question.

2. When an accused is held without bond, this means that the accused remains in jail from the time of arrest until the trial is over, hampering the accused's ability to aid in the preparation of a defense.

3. In this case, both sides had medical experts testify because the accused's sanity at the time of the crime for purposes of determining criminal responsibility was a critical issue on which expert medical testimony would be helpful and relevant.

4. Judges ordinarily use pattern jury instructions to instruct the jury on the law that they are required to follow in deciding the case. When a lawyer submits a special jury instruction to the court, the lawyer is requesting that the court instruct the jury on a legal issue that is either not covered, inadequately covered, or incorrectly covered in the pattern jury instructions. A special jury instruction may be submitted because the pattern instruction is confusing; because the law has changed; or in an effort to lay the groundwork for arguing on appeal that the law should be changed, as was done in this case.

5. After a jury verdict finding an accused guilty, in order to appeal, a lawyer must first ask the trial court to grant a new trial. To do so, the lawyer files a document known as a motion for new trial in which the lawyer lists all of the reasons that the accused is entitled to a new trial. The purpose of the motion is to give the trial judge the first opportunity to correct any errors. Usually, the trial judge will deny the motion.

If the accused appeals, the appellate court will consider only the issues that were raised in the motion, absent extraordinary circumstances.

Chapter X
State v. Mackey, 553 S.W.2d 337 (Tenn. 1977)

1. What constitutional rights does an accused surrender by pleading guilty to a criminal charge?

2. What must a judge do before accepting a guilty plea?

3. What is the purpose of requiring that trial judges adhere strictly to the *Mackey* guidelines when accepting an accused's guilty plea?

4. What is meant by a "voluntary" and "knowing" guilty plea?

5. What steps follow the entry of a guilty plea?

6. How does a guilty plea impact an accused's future?

7. What is meant by the phrase "collateral consequences?"

CHAPTER X

STATE v. MACKEY
553 S.W. 2d 337 (Tenn. 1977)

A former member of our firm, Ed Love, who primarily practiced civil law, was appointed to represent an indigent defendant in a case that, ultimately, would provide a framework for countless convicted individuals to argue that their convictions should be set aside.

Love was appointed to represent Andrew Mackey who, while awaiting trial on several charges, was charged with escaping from the custody of the Hamilton County Sheriff. Before Mackey could be tried on the felony escape charge, he was convicted of additional felonies, including armed robbery and rape.

Mackey decided to plead guilty on the escape charge but requested a jury to determine his punishment.[1] The judge did not ask Mackey any questions before accepting his guilty plea. During the trial on sentencing, Mackey did not testify. Notwithstanding defense counsel's pretrial and trial objections, the State was allowed to admit into evidence court records showing Mackey's prior convictions. In addition, over defense objection, a deputy sheriff was allowed to testify that Mackey attempted to escape a second time, during a recess in the trial. The jury sentenced Mackey to not less than one nor more than two years in the penitentiary.

Mackey appealed and the Tennessee Court of Criminal Appeals agreed with the defense argument that the judge should not have admitted evidence of Mackey's prior criminal convictions or testimony concerning Mackey's attempted escape during trial. The appellate court also agreed that Mackey's guilty plea on the charge of felony

---

1 Before July 1, 1982, defendants had a right to jury sentencing. Advisory Commission Comment, Tenn. R. Crim. P. 32(a). For offenses committed after July 1, 1982, Tennessee law provides that "the court shall set the sentence," except in limited circumstances, including capital cases. Tenn. R. Crim. P. 32(a).

escape had been involuntary because he plead guilty not knowing that the prior convictions would be allowed in evidence. The use of the prior conviction to enhance a subsequent sentence is what is known as a "collateral consequence" of pleading guilty. The appellate court held that the trial judge failed to investigate either the "voluntariness or intelligence" of Mackey's guilty plea. As a result, the guilty plea was set aside, and the case sent back for a new trial.

Not satisfied with that result, the prosecution asked the Tennessee Supreme Court to review the decision, likely recognizing the widespread impact of the lower appellate court's ruling. If Mackey's guilty plea was involuntary, what about countless other guilty pleas accepted by many other judges under similar or identical circumstances? If the prosecution's intent in seeking review was to moderate the procedures for accepting guilty pleas in Tennessee, the result they achieved was just the opposite.

The Tennessee Supreme Court affirmed the appellate court, relying on the United States Supreme Court's clear mandate in *Boykin v. Alabama*, 395 U.S. 238 (1969) and clarifying that before a guilty plea can be accepted, the trial court must address the accused on the record in open court and must inquire sufficiently to assure that the guilty plea is being entered voluntarily and intelligently. In Mackey's case, the judge did not ask any questions to determine that Mackey understood the consequences of his guilty plea. The Tennessee Supreme Court emphasized that a judge cannot assume that a guilty plea is intelligent and voluntary from a "silent record" such as the one in Mackey's case. *State v. Mackey*, 553 S.W.2d at 339-340 (citing and quoting *Boykin v. Alabama*, 395 U.S. at 242). Before the plea can be deemed intelligently and voluntarily entered, trial judges must assure that the accused understands the direct and collateral consequences of the guilty plea.

The decision in *Mackey* established the standard for trial judges to follow when accepting guilty pleas. The strict requirements, which have been incorporated into Rule 11 of the Tennessee Rules of Criminal Procedure, must be followed precisely. But the *Mackey* requirements are far more than a mechanical checklist. Rather, they are used to assure that an accused fully understands (1) the constitutional rights that are given up when a guilty plea is entered and (2) the potential collateral consequences of pleading guilty.

The court obviously wanted not only to apply but to amplify the constitutional requirement laid down in *Boykin*. In order to establish that a defendant is intelligently and voluntarily surrendering fundamental constitutional rights, the court must explain those rights and the defendant must waive those rights in open court. But the court also wanted to assure that a pleading defendant understood the future impact of a guilty plea. The court noted that while defendant's prior convictions might not have been admissible at trial, they were admissible at sentencing. "Therefore, the defendant should have been informed by the trial judge that such evidence would be admissible as a consequence of his entering a plea of guilty. Moreover, the record should affirmatively disclose that advice was imparted to the defendant before his plea of guilty was accepted." *State v. Mackey*, 553 S.W.2d at 341.

In this case, once again the work of a lawyer whose main practice area was civil law resulted in a landmark decision that expanded the constitutional rights and civil liberties of the accused. The decision of the Tennessee Supreme Court in *State v. Mackey* had far-reaching consequences. After *Mackey*, dozens of incarcerated individuals would succeed in setting aside prior guilty pleas and excluding evidence of prior convictions because the guilty plea proceeding did not indicate an intelligent and voluntary waiver of constitutional rights or an understanding of the consequences of pleading guilty.

What I Know

1. When an accused pleads guilty, the accused gives up several constitutional rights, including the right to plead not guilty and persist in that plea until found guilty beyond a reasonable doubt, the right to trial by jury, the right to confrontation, the right to be free from self-incrimination, the right to compel the attendance of witnesses, and the right to appeal.

2. The judge must determine whether the accused is knowingly and voluntarily pleading guilty. To satisfy the first requirement, the judge assures that the accused is aware of the constitutional rights that are being surrendered and the consequences of the guilty plea. To satisfy the voluntariness requirement, the judge asks questions to assure that the accused has not been threatened, coerced, or promised anything in exchange for the guilty plea. The judge must also ensure that there is a factual basis for the guilty plea before accepting the plea.

3. The purpose of requiring the strict adherence to the Mackey guidelines is to ensure that, before pleading guilty, the accused is advised by the judge of all the rights surrendered and potential consequences of pleading guilty.

4. A "voluntary" plea means a plea that is offered based on one's own free will, without coercion or other undue influence. A "knowing" plea is a plea that is entered by one who understands fully the rights surrendered and the likely direct and collateral consequences of the guilty plea.

5. After an accused has pled guilty, the accused will be sentenced by the judge. The actual sentence may be as a result of a negotiated plea agreement with the prosecutor or may be determined by the judge following a sentencing hearing at which the judge considers factors relevant to sentencing.

6. A guilty plea results in a conviction, the same as if the accused had been tried and convicted by a judge or jury. Convictions can be used against an accused in future criminal proceedings to enhance sentencing. In addition, an individual with criminal convictions faces a range of collateral consequences. These include limitations in employment and housing opportunities, the loss of the right to vote and hold certain public offices, and denial of some public benefits.

7. The phrase "collateral consequences" is used to refer to the consequences of a criminal conviction that are collateral to the sentence given for the crime. For example, collateral consequences may include court costs, losing the right to vote, losing the right to live in certain locations, having greater difficulty finding employment and, as in this case, being sentenced more harshly in the future because of prior convictions.

Chapter XI
Pace v. State, 566 S.W.2d 861 (Tenn. 1978)

1. What does it mean to challenge the constitutionality of a statute?

2. What are the underlying purposes of punishment for an individual who has been convicted of a crime?

3. Who determines the punishment for an individual convicted of a crime?

4. What role does the legislature (in Tennessee, the General Assembly) play in determining the sentencing policy of a state?

5. What alternatives to incarceration are used to punish convicted offenders?

6. What individual considerations should be considered in determining the appropriate punishment that an individual should receive?

7. How does public viewpoint impact sentencing?

8. How does economics impact sentencing?

CHAPTER XI

PACE v. STATE
566 S.W. 2d 861 (Tenn. 1978)

In 1975, the Tennessee General Assembly took a rare step and created a method for diverting certain criminal cases from the court system. The method, known as pretrial diversion, was prompted by a number of concerns, including the ineffectiveness and expense of the criminal legal system, in particular the growing costs of imprisonment.[1] Tennessee's pretrial diversion statute was amended in 1976 to require the trial court to dismiss charges "with prejudice" following the successful completion of a diversion program.[2]

---

1 In his concurring opinion in this case, Chief Justice Henry discussed the purpose and nature of pretrial diversion programs, indicating that the purpose "is to spare appropriately selected first offenders the stigma, embarrassment and expense of trial and the collateral consequences of a criminal conviction [with the] result contemplated [being] the restoration of successful divertees to useful and productive citizenship." *Pace v. State,* 566 S.W.2d 861, 868-69 (Tenn. 1978) (Henry, C.J., concurring).

2 The amendment to Tennessee Code Annotated §40-2105 (e) provided that

the trial court shall dismiss with prejudice any warrant or charge against the defendant upon the expiration of ninety (90) days after the expiration of the period of the suspension specified in the memorandum of understanding is filed [sic], provided no termination of the memorandum of understanding has been filed under the provision of subsection (d). If the prosecution is dismissed with prejudice, jeopardy shall attach, and the court shall make a minute entry to that effect.

Presently, Tennessee has two diversion statutes. Pretrial diversion, which requires prosecutorial approval, is available to "qualified defendants" as provided in Tennessee Code Annotated Section 40-15-105, while Tennessee Code Annotated Section 40-35-313 (a) (1) (A) provides for judicial diversion, by authorizing "[t]he court [to] defer further proceedings against a qualified defendant and place the defendant on probation upon such reasonable conditions as it may require without entering a judgment of guilty and with the consent of the qualified defendant." Both the pretrial and judicial diversion statutes provide for expungement of all public records following the successful completion of diversion. See Tenn. Code Ann. §§40-15-105(e); 40-35-313(b), but both require the payment of substantial fees to accomplish expungement.

Diversion was reserved for offenders who did not have prior felony convictions. My client, Carol Pace, who was indicted for fraudulent breach of trust in Hamilton County, was such an offender. As counsel for Pace, in accordance with Tennessee's pretrial diversion statute, I asked the district attorney to place Pace on pretrial diversion. Consistent with the opinion held by many prosecutors (and some judges) that a diversionary sentence was too "soft," the district attorney denied my request.

I then asked the trial judge in the case, the Honorable Joseph F. DiRisio, to review and overturn the prosecutor's decision. Judge DiRisio, who had served as an assistant district attorney before being elected as judge for the Criminal Court for Hamilton County, Division III, had the reputation for being a firm but fair judge. The judge was widely respected by attorneys who practiced before him, including me. I had previously practiced briefly with Judge DiRisio and Arvin Reingold after I left the Hamilton County District Attorney's office on January 1, 1969, before opening my own law office. We never had a dispute. While Joe DiRisio was probably the most organized attorney I have seen in all of my years of practice, Arvin Reingold, also a fine lawyer, was probably the least organized lawyer I have known. Together, they were a wonderful team for this young lawyer to work with in the beginning of his career and I learned valuable lessons from both of them. When Joe died at the early age of 69, I was honored to be one of his pallbearers. In addition to his organizational skills, Joe DiRisio was rumored to be one of the three most talented attorneys in his class at Vanderbilt Law School, a class that included Tennessee Supreme Court Justice William Harbison.

Prior to deciding whether to review and overturn the prosecutor's denial of diversion in the Pace case, Judge DiRisio called me into his office and placed a stack of papers in each of my hands, showing me that he had written two separate opinions. One decision upheld the validity of the pretrial diversion statute and the other declared the statute unconstitutional. The judge told me that he had not yet decided how he would rule, but wanted to make the right decision.

Ultimately, the trial judge held that portions of the pretrial diversion statute were unconstitutional on three grounds. First, the judge found the statute to be "incapable of coherent application" due to its vagueness and ambiguity; second, the statute violated a portion of the Tennessee Constitution related to the titles, or captions, of statutes; and third, the statute's provision requiring approval by the trial judge except in limited circumstances was an "impermissible invasion on the function of the judiciary." *Pace v. State*, 566 S.W.2d 861, 864 (Tenn. 1978). Because of the judge's ruling that the diversion statute was unconstitutional, Pace was tried, convicted, and sentenced to a suspended sentence.

Based on the judge's findings, and his consequent refusal to review my client's petition for pretrial diversion, I was able to appeal to the Tennessee Supreme Court. On appeal, I was ably supported by Robert Burch as amicus, on behalf of the Tennessee Association of Criminal Defense Lawyers (TACDL). A unanimous Tennessee Supreme Court reversed Judge DiRisio's decision and held that Tennessee's pretrial diversion statute was constitutional. On remand, Judge DiRisio placed Pace on pretrial diversion, she successfully completed her diversionary sentence, and the charges were ultimately removed from her record.

The good outcome in *Pace* presumably displeased the District Attorney General's Conference and some judges who called upon the Tennessee General Assembly to amend the pre-diversion statute. Over the course of time, several crippling modifications were adopted that diminished the usefulness of the statute and made it more difficult for offenders to receive its benefit.

For example, prosecutors vigorously opposed allowing pretrial diversion without the entry of a guilty plea, because in the event the diversion requirements were not successfully completed, the prosecution would have to begin the case anew, potentially after witnesses had become unavailable. Diversion that followed the entry of a guilty plea (that was held in abeyance) was more tolerable to prosecutors. If the accused successfully completed the diversionary program, the charge and plea would be expunged, that is removed from the defendant's record. But if the accused did not successfully complete the program, a conviction would be entered, and the accused would be sentenced in accordance with the plea agreement. In the decades since the *Pace* decision, the General Assembly has continued to decrease the opportunities for diversion in Tennessee and the courts have consistently emphasized that the prosecution has the discretion to determine whether to grant pretrial diversion.

Eligible offenders benefit greatly from diversion statutes. By maintaining a clean record, offenders avoid the numerous collateral consequences that follow a criminal conviction.[3] They are able to secure better employment, have more satisfactory careers, and live more productive lives.

Because of the continued rising costs of jailing and imprisoning individuals, the trend should be toward removing as many non-violent offenders as possible from the penal system. This would be a move in the right direction. Unfortunately, given the current political climate, it should be anticipated that the availability of diversion statutes will be restricted even further.

---

3 The collateral consequences of a conviction are far-reaching. For example, in Tennessee, currently convictions for driving under the influence (DUI) cannot be expunged. Having a criminal record may adversely affect employment opportunities.

What I Know

1 To challenge the constitutionality of a statute means to argue that the statute violates provisions of either the state or federal constitution or both. If a statute is unconstitutional, it is invalid and cannot be applied.

2. Punishment of a crime serves several purposes for the offender, the victim, and the public. Punishment can rehabilitate offenders, allowing them to re-enter society with a stronger resolve to live a law-abiding life. Alternatively, the experience of being charged and convicted of a crime may be so unpleasant that the offender decides against (is deterred from) reoffending to avoid further punishment. Punishing offenders also vindicates the rights of victims and, in some situations, can help protect victims from further harm. Further, punishment communicates societal values and may deter criminal activity in the first place. Punishment may accomplish one or several of these goals at a time.

3. Punishment is generally decided by judges, except in capital cases, in which the accused has a right to jury sentencing. Judges will consider many factors, including the circumstances of the case, the offender's criminal history, the victim's opinion, sentencing guidelines adopted by the legislature, and more.

4. The legislature creates general sentencing provisions for judges to follow. Historically, judges had wide discretion in punishing offenders. However, legislatures have limited judicial power somewhat by enacting sentencing guidelines, mandatory minimum sentences, and other similar laws. These sentencing provisions may be influenced by statistical data, previous criminal laws, and public policy.

5. Judges can impose several types of punishments depending on the specific state or federal law. Judges may require an offender to pay a

fine, and/or restitution, to complete community service, to attend rehabilitation or treatment programs, to be subjected to the rules of and supervision by probation, to be restricted by electronic monitoring equipment, to be confined except during work hours (work release), or to be incarcerated for the duration of the sentence. Some states also authorize capital punishment for felony murder and first-degree murder.

6. Courts may have leeway to adjust a sentence based on mitigating or aggravating factors. The judge will likely examine the defendant's background, including age, family history, educational background, prior criminal history, and medical history. The judge will also look at the nature of the offense, the harm imposed, and whether there are mitigating factors, such as mental or physical infirmities, that contributed to the offense. Judges will also look at the facts of the case to understand what sentence will result in the best outcomes for the offender, victim, and public. Sentencing may also be influenced by the defendant's response to the crime. Remorseful offenders and those who accept responsibility for their offenses may receive less severe sentences than criminals who are indifferent or uncooperative.

7. Public opinion affects what factors the legislature incorporates into statutory sentencing guidelines and the length of sentences that the legislature imposes. For example, in many states, simple possession of marijuana has either been decriminalized or treated similarly to traffic infractions, while in others, the public opinion has led the legislature to continue to provide criminal sanctions, including a fine or imprisonment, for the crime. Public opinion may also influence a judge's sentencing decision as when, for example, a judge feels pressure due to an escalating crime rate or a rash of particular types of crime in the judge's jurisdiction. Judges may take into account public opinion, but only within the bounds of the law.

8. The criminal justice system accounts for a significant percentage of government expenditures. Policing, prosecuting, supervising, and incarcerating all require a tremendous expenditure of government resources. Thus, many reformists suggest that economics should be considered as a key, if not dominant, factor in determining the length and method of punishment.

Chapter XII
State v. Franklin, 714 S.W.2d 252 (Tenn. 1986)

1. What is the role of a lawyer who has been appointed to represent an unpopular client?

2. How does a lawyer separate personal values and beliefs from those of the lawyer's clients?

3. What is "pro se" representation?

4. Why should an accused have the right to self-representation?

5. What is the role of counsel when a client refuses to follow counsel's advice?

6. What is "hybrid representation?" How did hybrid representation occur in this case?

7. What are the likely reasons that counsel objected to the client's request to give a closing statement to the jury in this case?

8. In at attorney-client relationship, which decisions are made by the client and which decisions are made by the lawyer?

9. In this case, why would the lawyers appeal the client's conviction after the client told the jury that he committed the crime?

CHAPTER Xll

STATE v. FRANKLIN
714 S.W. 2d 252 (Tenn. 1986)

One of the most difficult cases in my legal career was my representation of accused anti-Semitic segregationist, white supremacist, and serial killer Joseph Paul Franklin. Along with former Assistant United States Attorney Hugh Moore, I was appointed to represent Franklin who was charged with the bombing of the Beth Shalom Synagogue in Chattanooga. The synagogue was completely destroyed in an explosion that occurred on July 29, 1977, just before 9:00 p.m. The investigation revealed that explosives, located in the crawl space beneath the center of the building, were ignited by electricity via a two hundred feet long extension cord plugged into an outside socket at a nearby motel. During the investigation, investigators noted the strong odor of exploded dynamite. But almost seven years elapsed before Joseph Franklin was charged in the bombing.

In 1984, Franklin was incarcerated at the maximum-security federal prison in Marion, Illinois, for unrelated murders. At Marion, inmates were locked up twenty-three hours of the day and placed in solitary confinement without any contact with other prisoners whenever there was a threat or attempt on an inmate's life. Because Franklin had been attacked and stabbed by other inmates, he was isolated from the general prison's population in a special housing unit.

While at Marion, Franklin evidently talked about the Chattanooga synagogue bombing, leading an officer from the Bureau of Alcohol, Tobacco and Firearms (BATF) and a detective from the Chattanooga Police Department to visit him. On February 29, 1984, while at Marion, Franklin confessed to the bombing and other crimes, including the shooting of Vernon Jordan, President of the National Urban League. Franklin told the investigators that he had intended the bomb to explode during mid-week services, when the synagogue was full, but he had miscalculated the time. Franklin openly condemned mixed raced couples, Jewish people, and other minorities.

Franklin was tried in Chattanooga before Criminal Court Judge Doug Meyer from July 10-12, 1984. The prosecution established that Franklin had obtained dynamite from a Chattanooga supply store in late June 1977, and another explosive, Tovex, from a Charleston, West Virginia, supplier in early July 1977 using his alias, James Clayton Vaughan. Fingerprints from the BATF explosives transaction records of sales were compared to Franklin's known fingerprints and positively identified as a match. The signatures on records were also determined to be Franklin's.

To explain Franklin's confession and to defend against this mountain of circumstantial evidence, the defense readily admitted that the defendant had confessed to the bombing, but claimed that the confession was untruthful, motivated by Franklin's desire to be transferred from Marion's tough solitary confinement conditions to a facility where he might serve his sentence in a less hostile environment (or, perhaps have a better chance to escape). The defense argued that Franklin learned the details of the bombing through numerous newspaper accounts but that he did not actually commit the crime.

To bolster the defense, we presented the testimony of a Lawrenceville, Georgia police officer, John Cowart, who had investigated the shooting of Hustler publisher, Larry Flynt. During his investigation, Cowart talked to Franklin in December 1983. Franklin confessed to shooting Flynt, but when Franklin confessed his role in the Beth Shalom Synagogue bombing to the BATF in February 1984, he had specifically denied shooting Flynt.

As a defense witness, Cowart provided damaging testimony to the prosecution's case, recalling that Franklin told him that he would cooperate with Officer Cowart if Cowart would try to "help get [him] out of [Marion]." Franklin then confessed to attempting to kill Flynt. Cowart also recalled that Franklin said, "I'll tell you I'm getting to a point now where I'd say anything to get out of here for a while." *State v. Franklin*, 714 S.W.2d at 255.

In order to convey the horrendous circumstances of Franklin's living conditions at Marion, I questioned Officer Cowart about violence against Franklin, including Franklin's stabbing, and about an attempt to sexually assault him with a steel pipe, information we had received from what we thought was a legitimate source. Franklin reacted immediately, denying the events had ever happened; from that point forward, he and I were unable to get along.

Both sides rested their case on July 12, 1984 and presented closing arguments. The prosecution argued that Franklin had been motivated by his political and religious beliefs and that those beliefs were corroborated by his confession. Hugh Moore gave the first part of the defense's closing argument, arguing that the defendant deserved a fair trial on the charges and emphasizing that he was not being tried for his political beliefs.

After Hugh finished his argument and just before I began my part of the closing argument, Franklin indicated that he wanted to make a closing statement to the jury. We objected to his doing so, fearing what he might say. The judge conducted a hearing out of the presence of the jury and overruled our objections, but told to the jury that:

> "Members of the jury, Mr. Franklin has requested that he be allowed to represent himself as far as a closing statement to the jury. I caution you that his statement is a statement. It is not testimony. It is not sworn testimony. He is merely acting as his own attorney, which he has the right to do, in making a closing statement to you. It is not evidence."

Franklin began by telling the jury that his statement was "unrehearsed" and that he had "just recently decided to make this statement, within the hour." After commenting about being stabbed while at Marion, Franklin stated: "I want to make your job a little easier here, as far as your deliberations go. You know, I admit to you that I bombed the synagogue. You know, I did it. You know, and I'll tell it to anybody around. It was a synagogue of Satan." He explained his reasoning for the bombing, connecting it to his interpretations of the Bible, quoting the Bible, and reading portions of the book of Revelation.

He outlined his belief that the Jewish people controlled the American government, the media, the communist nations, and the western democracies and were "trying to destroy [the white race] through race mixing and through communism." *Id.* at 256. Franklin closed with his proposal: "the only way that the white race can be saved now and get out of the trouble that they're in today, is for everybody to fast and get on their knees and praise the Lord. And I just hope that everybody here does that and accepts Jesus Christ as their personal savior." *Id.*

Although I had prepared what I thought was a good closing argument, it was time to improvise. Following the shocking experience of hearing my client's confession and sermon to the jury, I had the unique task of presenting my closing argument for the defense. I stressed that given the defendant's beliefs, affording the defendant a fair trial was of paramount importance. I told the jury to "put aside any feelings that [they] have in regard to whether [they] agree[d] or disagree[d] with him... and make [the] decision on the facts of this case." I continued: "I don't think you're ever [going to] see any two lawyers in the position probably ... where really we're asking you to not believe our client and the D.A.'s asking you to believe him." *Id.* at 256-57. I explained to the jury that without the defendant's confession, he would not have been a suspect; furthermore, given his lengthy prison sentences, which we had admitted to the jury, he had "nothing to lose in confessing [and he] had used the trial as a forum to express his political and religious views." *Id.* at 257.

The prosecution, in their final closing argument, told the jury that "[t]he motive for being here in this trial is the same motive for the explosion of the synagogue.... He wants attention for his attitudes and feelings, his warped, demented thinking about races of people." *Id.* Ultimately, the jury convicted Franklin, and he was sentenced to 15-21 years for the bombing and 6-10 years for possession of explosives with the sentences to be served consecutive to each other.

In our efforts to receive a new trial, we argued that Franklin had acted against our advice in making the closing statement to the jury and that the trial judge had erred in permitting him to act as his own counsel, particularly since Franklin had never requested to serve as his own counsel. The trial court denied our motion for a new trial and summarized the unique circumstances of the case in this manner:

> As you said, this is a novel situation. This is where a defendant insisted, and the Court allowed him to be his own attorney. And the reason the contrary is not true is that the defendant has a constitutional right to be his own lawyer. So, if you give him that right then it's not error then for – I don't see how the Court can be in error if he allows him to be his own attorney. All I'm doing is allowing him to exercise his constitutional right to be his own lawyer. I cannot force an attorney upon him. I do have a right I guess to protect a defendant from himself. But when you observe the defendant and you realize the defendant is doing what he wants to do, that the defendant is sane, that the defendant is making a knowing decision on his part, then I have no right really to cut off his constitutional right. And having observed Mr. Franklin several days in the course of the trial, I realized that he was capable of representing himself. He was conducting the trial the way he wanted the trial to be conducted. And, of course, it's obvious that he did not agree with the line of defense that his attorneys were setting out. But I think he had that right to get up and argue the case the way he wanted to.

Id. at 258. Additionally, the trial court observed that Franklin made the independent decisions to absent himself periodically from the courtroom, Franklin asked before trial that his shackles be removed, and Franklin read the Bible throughout trial while following along with the proceedings.

In the opinion of the Tennessee Court of Criminal Appeals, the trial court had failed to determine the validity of the defendant's waiver of the right to counsel, which is required before self-representation can be undertaken. In reversing Franklin's, conviction, the intermediate appellate court held that "while a defendant has an alternative right to counsel or to elect self-representation, he has no right to both at once, unless the interest of justice requires it." *Id.* at 263.

Dissatisfied with this result, the prosecution requested that the Tennessee Supreme Court grant permission to appeal to address the validity of "hybrid representation" – whether an accused may be both self-represented and represented by counsel. The procedure that was followed in Franklin's case was approved due to the unique circumstances, but the court spent most of the opinion outlining precise steps that a trial judge must follow when confronted with hybrid representation requests. As a preliminary matter, the judge must determine that the defendant "is not seeking to disrupt the trial" and that the defendant has the "intelligence, ability and general competence to participate in his own defense." *Id.* at 260. Additionally, hybrid representation should not be allowed except in "exceptional circumstances" that justify the request and that are described on the record. Before the defendant participates in this manner, the defendant must have an opportunity to confer privately with counsel and must be told not to "state facts not in evidence." *Id.* Finally, the defendant and the jury must be told that "the defendant is acting as his own counsel and that the defendant is not giving any evidence or testimony." *Id.* In all due respect, it is worth noting that several of the above requirements were not followed in Franklin's case; given the notoriety of the defendant, apparently relief from his conviction was not going to be granted.

When we were appointed to represent Franklin, we could not have predicted that his case would ultimately result in the Tennessee Supreme Court providing a framework for trial judges confronted with hybrid representation requests. Nor could we anticipate that the framework the court adopted in *Franklin* would inform their decision several years later on an equally important right of the accused – whether the accused has waived the right to testify. Though *State v. Franklin* is never cited in the case of *Momon v. State*, 18 S.W.3d 152 (Tenn. 1999), the importance of the accused's individual autonomy in choosing to testify, as in requesting to self-represent, is emphasized by Justice Drowota, who authored both opinions.

The right to self-represent, to remain silent, or to testify, all guarded by the United States Constitution, can sometimes lead to unusual and disastrous results. The *Franklin* case demonstrates the need for defense counsel to remain alert for any change in circumstances that may necessitate a change in trial strategy. As a post-script to the case, it is ironic that when I ran into a member of the jury sometime later, the juror informed me that "until Franklin took the stand there was a good possibility that the jury was going to turn him loose."

What I Know

1. It is a lawyer's job to be an advocate. A lawyer ensures that their client is well-represented and that their rights are maintained and protected; ultimately, a lawyer's task is to assure that the client receives due process of law. This can be difficult personally for the lawyer when the client is unpopular, but it is important to remember that justice cannot be accomplished, and our adversary system of justice cannot work, unless everyone has a right to effective representation by counsel.

2. A lawyer's personal values and beliefs are separate from and not implicated by a lawyer's representation of a client. While lawyers generally can choose who to represent, the lawyer's professional conduct rules provide that all lawyers have a "responsibility" of assisting in pro bono and court-appointed cases and to do so "by accepting a fair share of unpopular maters or indigent or unpopular clients." Tenn. R. Prof. Conduct 6.2, Comment [1].

3. The phrase "pro se" is Latin for "in one's own behalf." In this case, the client attempted to represent himself at the end of his trial by asking to make a closing statement on his own behalf, although he was represented by counsel.

4. The Sixth Amendment provides that "[i]n all criminal prosecutions, the accused shall enjoy the right ... to have the Assistance of Counsel for the defence." U.S. Const. amend. VI. The right to counsel does not prohibit an accused from proceeding without counsel and conducting his or her own defense provided that the court finds that the accused has the ability to self-represent. Allowing self-representation is based on the premise of individual autonomy, that the accused should be in control of the defense of the case since it is the accused whose life is impacted by the prosecution. In some circumstances, the

court will appoint "standby counsel" to assist a client who has invoked the right to self-representation.

5. A lawyer has a duty to communicate advice in a manner that enables the client to understand and act upon the advice. But, in the end, a lawyer cannot force a client to take advice. If a client refuses to adhere to counsel's advice, on a significant issue, the lawyer may request permission to withdraw from representing the client, but the judge decides whether to allow counsel to withdraw.

6. "Hybrid representation" is the phrase that refers to circumstances in which an accused has counsel but also actively participates in presenting his or her own defense. In this case, hybrid representation occurred when the trial court allowed the accused and both of his appointed counsel to give closing arguments.

7. Counsel likely objected to the trial court allowing the accused to give a pro se closing argument because counsel was unable to predict and feared what the accused would say. They may have expected that the accused's statements would include his political and religious opinions and that those opinions would likely offend, frighten, or prejudice the jury. Ultimately, counsel's fears and concerns, which led to their objection, were realized when the accused gave his closing statement.

8. In the course of representation, the client sets the overall goals of the representation. The lawyer's role is to decide on the best course of action to achieve the client's goals and take those actions. In a criminal case, the client always has the right to decide whether to plead guilty or not guilty, whether to waive the right to a trial by jury, and whether to testify at trial.

9. A court-appointed lawyer has an obligation in all but the most extraordinary circumstances to aid the client in exercising the right to appeal. In this case, the lawyers likely appealed the conviction because of their belief that allowing Franklin to make a closing statement interfered with Franklin's fair trial rights and potentially prejudiced the jury against Franklin. Counsel may also have appealed based on their belief that Franklin was not capable of self-representation.

Chapter XIII
Summers v. Thompson
764 S.W.2d 182 (Tenn.), *reh. denied*, (Tenn. 1988)

1. How are courts created?

2. Who determines the jurisdiction of a court?

3. What does "independence of the judiciary" mean?

4. What is the interplay between the doctrine of separation of powers and the principle of judicial independence?

5. How does political pressure impact the courts?

6. How are the concepts of separation of powers, judicial independence, and political pressure illustrated in the *Summers v. Thompson* case?

7. How does a state decide how to choose its judges?

8. What are the various judicial selection methods and some of the pros and cons of each?

CHAPTER XIII

SUMMERS v. THOMPSON
764 S.W. 2d 182 (Tenn.), *reh. denied*, (Tenn. 1988)

The twin cities of Soddy-Daisy were separate communities prior to 1969, when the municipality in the northern end of Hamilton County was formed to prevent Chattanooga and Hamilton County from annexing the area. The Soddy-Daisy government structure consisted of a mayor and a board of commissioners. The Soddy-Daisy Board of Commissioners appointed a city attorney and city judge. From its creation, the Soddy-Daisy City Court's jurisdiction authorized the city judge to conduct trials on misdemeanor charges, imposing fines up to fifty dollars ($50) and imposing jail sentences up to eleven months and twenty-nine days (11-29) in the workhouse or county jail. The city judge could also hear preliminary hearings in criminal cases and set bail bonds in more serious, felony, cases. In rare cases, the city judge could dismiss felony charges, but the district attorney could present the dismissed charges to a grand jury, which could recharge the accused for trial in criminal court.

In 1971, at age thirty, I was appointed by the Soddy-Daisy Board of Commissioners to serve as the Soddy-Daisy City Judge. The late Glen McColpin was appointed to serve as the first Soddy-Daisy City Attorney. As judge, I was paid three hundred dollars ($300) a month. My duties included holding court in the north end of the county twice a month and being available for calls at all hours of the night. Both Glen and I were considered "at will" employees serving at the pleasure of the Soddy-Daisy mayor and the four commissioners.

I had served in the position for fourteen years when, on October 3, 1985, at a regular board meeting, I was terminated without cause and without notice. When the citizens pressed for an explanation of why I was terminated, the mayor and commissioners refused to respond. This incensed the citizens, with a majority disagreeing with my termination. Some speculated that the "Board intended to turn the city court into a "cash register court." *Summers v. Thompson*, 764 S.W.2d 182, 183 (Tenn. 1988). The termination itself did not trouble be, but the manner and circumstances of the termination did.

After I was fired, a group of angry citizens urged me to sue the city of Soddy-Daisy to be reinstated as city judge. In an effort to resolve the matter, I told the citizen group that if they obtained 2,500 registered voters' signatures on a petition, (a number I thought would be impossible to get) I would sue and donate any back pay I received to one of the local charities that served those with mental and physical disabilities. Unfortunately, I underestimated the support and enthusiasm of my friends in Soddy-Daisy. They secured almost 3,000 signatures! I had been outsmarted and had to sue.

The case of *Summers v. Thompson* went to trial before the Honorable Vann Owens, Chancellor of the Hamilton County Chancery Court with myself, the late Jack Brown and the late Robert L. Moon as my counsel at trial and on appeal. The basis of my claim was that the Tennessee statute that allowed termination of a judicial officer at will violated the Tennessee Constitution and offended the principle of separation of powers. Chancellor Owens agreed, holding that "judicial independence and impartiality could not be assured if the city judge had no definite term and was subjected to the whims of the local legislative body... . " *Id.* at 184. In addition to declaring the statute to be unconstitutional, Chancellor Owens ordered my reinstatement as city judge.

Mayor Lynn Thompson and the Soddy-Daisy Board of Commission appealed. Because the sole determinative issue was the constitutionality of state statutes, the appeal went directly to the Tennessee Supreme Court. Once again, the Tennessee Association of Criminal Defense Lawyers (TACDL) responded by filing an amicus curiae brief; the brief was authored by Deborah S. Swettenam. The Tennessee Trial Lawyers Association (TTLA) also came to my aid with J. Anthony Farmer doing an excellent job, authoring their amicus brief.

The Supreme Court opinion, authored by Justice Frank Drowota, summarized the facts and outlined the cause of the friction between the parties. In the majority's words:

[a]pparently, the Mayor and members of the Board attempted to influence the judicial functions of the city court by attempting to utilize the court to increase city revenue, by requesting that the authority to issue warrants be delegated to city officers or employees who were not magistrates, and by seeking to establish a fixed schedule for appearance bonds, which would be set by clerks. In addition, Mayor Thompson attempted to persuade Petitioner to impose harsher sentences on first offenders in cases involving driving under the influence but Petitioner resisted, contending that judicial discretion was involved in determining the appropriate punishment within the ranges permitted by statute. Evidently, when the Mayor and Board concluded that Petitioner could not be persuaded to conduct city court in the manner in which they wished, they concluded that the at will employment statute could be utilized to terminate Petitioner and replace him with a more malleable city judge.

Id. at 1.

Although both parties and the trial judge had assumed the application of the same statutes, the Tennessee Supreme Court held that the statutes in question were misapplied. Applying the correct statute, the court concluded that the Soddy-Daisy City Court was not a court vested with the same jurisdiction as inferior courts in Tennessee, but rather was a court with jurisdiction "wholly limited to traffic violations or violations of city ordinances." *Id.* at 184. Consequently, judges in these jurisdictions are "essentially administrative judges," *Id.* at 183, and do not exercise "constitutional judicial power." *Id.* at 185. Thus the Soddy-Daisy Board of Commissioners was authorized to remove me at will and without cause.

In what is likely the only opinion of its kind in the annals of Tennessee appellate jurisprudence, Justice Drowota authored not only the majority opinion, but also a lengthy concurring opinion, in which he expressed his discomfort with the application of the "at will" doctrine to judges. In straightforward language, Justice Drowota declared that the "protection of constitutional rights does not depend on the type of court before which a person may be brought." *Id.* at 194 (Drowota, J., concurring). His concurrence seemed to invite litigants to raise the issue in different circumstances such as, for example, when the court at issue was vested with the same jurisdiction as that of Tennessee's inferior courts. And, that is, in fact, what happened.

Four years later, the Tennessee Supreme Court decided a case concerning the jurisdiction of the Municipal Court of the Town of South Carthage. That case, the court concluded, was "controlled by ... Justice Drowota's concurring opinion in *Summers v. Thompson* ... ." *Town of South Carthage v. Barrett*, 840 S.W.2d 895 (Tenn. 1992). Ultimately, the Supreme Court adopted Justice Drowota's "inherent logic."

> [i]f the Legislature extends the jurisdiction of [a city court] to include enforcement of any State statutes, constitutional judicial power is vested in them under Article VI [of the Tennessee Constitution] because the city court then exercises a concurrent jurisdiction with an inferior court. Therefore, in order to serve 'one of the most fundamental principles of American constitutional government, an independent judiciary, ... city judges properly exercising any concurrent jurisdiction with an inferior court must be elected for a term of eight (8) years as required by Article VI, Section 4, and may not be removed except pursuant to the Constitution of Tennessee.

Id. at 898 (internal citations omitted) (quoting *Summers v. Thompson*, 764 S.W.2d at 199 (Drowota, J., concurring)).

I lost the case against the Soddy-Daisy Mayor and Board of Commissioners and my judicial career was over, but my case and the *Town of South Carthage* case that followed illuminated the political pressure that can occur in small municipalities where a city judge serves at the will of a board or commission. The loss of three hundred dollars ($300) a month salary to shed light on that dynamic was well worth it! Moreover, the maxim of "taking one for the team" is directly applicable to my case. In the Town of South Carthage case, the Tennessee Supreme Court noted that my case "aptly demonstrates the danger posed to an independent judiciary and the impartial administration of justice through the exercise of arbitrary power by a separate branch of the government motivated by policy and political concerns inimical to an independent system of justice. Judicial independence is essential to the effective operation of constitutional government." *Id.* at 899. Although removing all politics from any judicial office is not possible, these two decisions advanced the cause of judicial independence by placing the question of whether to remove a judge in the hands of the voters.

What I Know

1. Courts are created either by the federal or state constitutions, by federal, state, or local legislative bodies, or by municipal charters.

2. Jurisdiction refers to the authority of a court to hear and determine certain types of cases. A court's jurisdiction is established, generally, in the document that creates the court, be that a constitution, a statute, or a municipal charter or ordinance.

3. "Independence of the judiciary" refers to the principle that courts should decide cases based on the law and the facts without being improperly influenced by other branches of government, politics, public pressure, financial influences, or other special interests.

4. The doctrine of separation of powers and the principle of judicial independence combined attempt to assure that courts will act independently from the other branches; will not bow to pressure or intimidation from the legislative and executive branches to uphold legislative or executive actions; will not be swayed by political and public pressure; and will rule based upon what the constitution and the law requires.

5. When judges are subject to partisan selection methods, there is concern that the judges will feel pressured to align with the ideologies of the political party and base decisions on what the political party wants rather than on what the law requires. Partisanship that influences a judge destroys the integrity, undermines the independence, and defeats the purpose of the judicial system.

6. This case illustrated a conflict between the separation of powers and the independence of the judiciary. The executive (mayor) and legislative (commission) branches attempted to influence the work of the city court (judiciary) by pressuring the city judge to impose higher

fines and harsher penalties, despite the fact that the judge had the sole authority to determine the appropriate sentence. When the judge refused to submit to the political pressure exerted by the other branches, he was fired, an example of the executive and legislative branches exerting power over the judicial branch.

7. In each state, the method of judicial selection is set out in either the state constitution, state law, or both.

8. State judges are either elected or appointed. Elections may be partisan, non-partisan, or retention elections. Those who favor elections believe that elections keep judges more responsive to the citizens and give the citizens a greater role in determining who becomes a judge. This direct accountability is also a downside of electing judges because it may cause judges to succumb to the will of the majority. Those who favor appointed systems claim that appointed systems produce a more highly qualified and diverse judiciary, while elections favor the candidates who raise the most money; moreover, in addition to the skyrocketing expense of judicial elections, campaign messages often mislead the public as to the role of the judge, suggesting that judges, like other politicians, rule based on personal and political ideologies rather than following the rule of law.

Chapter XIV
State v. Freeman, Criminal Court of Hamilton County, Tennessee (1993)

1. What was the likely reason that the framers of the Tennessee Constitution provided for fixed judicial salaries during the term of office?

2. What is the effect of connecting a judge's salary to results in cases?

3. What is an en banc hearing? Why was one likely requested in this case?

4. What concerns were raised by the fee-generating practices outlined in this case?

5. What is the process for creating new courts or new judgeships?

6. Why can a judge's position not be eliminated during a judge's term of office?

7. How does this case illustrate the importance of unique provisions in state constitutions?

CHAPTER XIV

STATE v. FREEMAN
CRIMINAL COURT OF HAMILTON COUNTY
Divisions 1-3 (1993)

The defendant, Ron Freeman, was arrested by the Chattanooga Police Department and charged with driving under the influence of an intoxicant and two traffic charges, both of which were violations of city ordinances. The city ordinance violations were set to be heard by Chattanooga City Court Judge Walter Williams. Williams, a judge elected to serve an eight-year term, had recently appeared before the Chattanooga City Council (the governing body of the City of Chattanooga) to request a pay raise. To substantiate his request, Judge Williams claimed that he had produced over one million dollars ($1,000,000) in revenue for the city treasury, by using his powers as a judicial officer to fine individuals who appeared before him in amounts up to one thousand dollars ($1,000) per case. This was in direct contravention of a provision of the Tennessee Constitution that required that all fines exceeding fifty dollars ($50) be assessed by a jury. Tenn. Const. Art. VI, section 14.[1] Although attorneys from the City Attorney's office were present during Judge William's presentation to the Chattanooga City Council, they did not raise an objection. After congratulating Judge Williams on his revenue raising efforts, the City Council approved a substantial pay raise.

When Ron Freeman's case came before Judge Williams, I requested that the case be dismissed because the Chattanooga City Court was acting without jurisdiction in light of Judge Williams' receipt of an illegal pay raise during the term of his office. My argument was based on the Tennessee Constitution, which provides as follows:

---

1 The Tennessee courts have held that when an individual waives the right to trial by jury, that waiver includes a waiver of the right to have a jury assess all fines in excess of fifty dollars ($50). See *State v. Harless,* 607 S.W. 2d 492 (Tenn. Crim. App. 1980).

The Judges of the Supreme or Inferior Courts,[2] shall, at stated times, receive a compensation for their serves, to be ascertained by law, which shall not be increased or diminished during the time for which they are elected. They shall not be allowed any fees or perquisites of office nor hold any other office of trust or profit under the State or the United States.

Tenn. Const. Art. VI, section 7. As the Tennessee Supreme Court noted in 1915, quoting the Federalist Papers, "next to permanency in office, nothing could contribute more to the independence of the judges than a fixed appropriation for their support." *State v. Brown*, 179 S.W. 321, 322 (Tenn. 1915) (quoting *The Judges' Salary Case*, 75 S.W. 1061, 1065 (Tenn. 1903).

Our motion to dismiss also raised constitutional issues pertaining to the doctrine of the separation of powers, the right to be tried before a neutral and detached magistrate, the right to a fair trial under both the federal and state constitutions, and the right to a jury in cases involving fines of more than fifty dollars ($50).

As expected, Judge Williams overruled our motion to dismiss but allowed us, with the agreement of the District Attorney's office, to appeal to the Hamilton County Criminal Court. During the pendency of the appeal, the Hamilton County Public Defender, Ardena Garth, intervened in the case to protect the interests of two of her appointed clients.

Next, our office requested that the three judges of the Hamilton County Criminal Court, Judge Douglas A. Meyer, Judge Joseph F. DiRisio, and Judge Steven Bevil, sit en banc, meaning siting as a panel, for the purpose of seeking a uniform order that would apply in all three courts because of the number of cases that could be impacted by the ruling. To my surprise, the three judges on March 22, 1993, agreed to sit en banc and scheduled a hearing for oral argument on May 3, 1993.

---

2 The City Court of Chattanooga was given concurrent jurisdiction with the Justice of the Peace Courts (now General Sessions Courts) by Private Act in 1936 to try state misdemeanor cases with sentences of up to eleven months and twenty-nine (11-29) days in the workhouse and to have preliminary hearings in felony cases.

On June 3, the three judges issued separate opinions, resulting in a 2-1 ruling and an Order remanding the case back to the Chattanooga City Court.

Judge Joe DiRisio, in his opinion, stated:

> Obviously beyond question is the conclusion that the salary increase was unconstitutional and in violation of Article VI sec[tion] 7 as well as a violation of the doctrine of separation of powers and the requirement of the neutral and detached magistrate.

Judge Stephen Bevil stated:

> The granting of a salary increase to Judge Williams during his term of office is unconstitutional, but it does not affect his qualification for office.

Judge Doug Meyer stated in his opinion that:

> The granting of salary increases during their term of office of the city judges may or may not violate Article VI, section 7 of the Tennessee Constitution [but] did not violate the doctrine of separation of powers of Article Il, section I of the Tennessee Constitution and the [other] constitutional violations cited in this pleading.

Judge Meyer further commented that the Criminal Court did not have all of the proof necessary to decide the case.

The June 3 order and the opinion of at least two of the judges of the Hamilton County Criminal Court that Judge William's pay raise was illegal, concerned District Attorney General Gary Gerbitz. Gerbitz directed the Chattanooga Police Department to take all cases in which the violation of a state law was charged to the General Sessions Court of Hamilton County rather than to the City Court of Chattanooga. Before the directive, the two Chattanooga City Courts were handling approximately seventy to eighty percent (70-80 %) of those cases, meaning that compliance would result in a significant increase in the number of cases to be heard by the three Hamilton County General Sessions Court judges, who were also responsible for handing the civil cases filed in that court.

Needless to say, chaos reigned. The general sessions courts were unprepared to handle such an influx in cases because of a lack of courtroom space, courtroom personnel, and judges to try the cases. During this time period, the opinion previously held by members of the legal profession that the general sessions judgeship was the easiest judicial job at the courthouse began to change.

When Judge Meyer learned of District Attorney Gerbitz's actions, he issued a second opinion, criticizing the directive, questioning his authority to "order" the officers of the Chattanooga Police Department to "do anything" or to interfere with the operation of the Chattanooga City Court, and urging Gerbitz to petition the Tennessee Court of Criminal Appeals to "stay" the June 3 Order issued by his fellow judges. Despite Judge Meyer's protests, the cases began to be moved to the general sessions courts.

The City of Chattanooga did not object to the new policy, primarily because it enabled the city to close the antiquated city jail, which was serving as a holding area for individuals facing city court charges who could not make bail. The removal of the cases also eliminated the city's potential liability for jail injuries and an annual cost to taxpayers in excess of one million dollars ($1,000,000). Once the cases were shifted, the dirty courtroom was renovated and converted into a modern city council auditorium with enlarged public capacity.

Because the Tennessee General Assembly was not in session at the time of these changes, no new judges could be appointed to help with the influx of cases in the Hamilton County General Sessions courts. To accommodate the large dockets of cases, lawyers were appointed to serve as special judges, and although most served fairly and impartially, a few used the opportunity to solicit business. One even heard some cases in which the prosecuting police officer was a divorce client. Eventually, the Tennessee General Assembly created two new judgeships for the Hamilton County General Sessions courts, and Ron Durby and Bob Moon were appointed to serve until the next general election.

The decision that outlawed Judge Williams' practice of setting fines in excess of fifty dollars ($50) without a jury in violation of the

Tennessee Constitution was never appealed. City court became primarily a traffic ticket court and efforts were made to reduce it to a single division. Ironically, the same provision of the Tennessee Constitution, Article VI, Section 7, used to challenge Judge William's jurisdiction guaranteed the other city judges, Judge Russell Bean and Judge Sherry Paty, job tenure through the end of their elected term of office. In 2021, the Chattanooga City Council passed an ordinance that will eliminate the second division of the city court following the expiration of the eight-year term of the judge elected in August 2022.

Once again, the Tennessee Constitution, drafted in 1796, was used effectively to curb an illegal practice and ensure the fairness and impartiality of the courts.

What I Know

1. The framers of the Tennessee Constitution required that a judge's salary remain fixed during the term of office to promote judicial independence, limiting the ability of the legislature to either award or punish a judge based on the judge's rulings.

2. Connecting a judge's salary to case outcomes creates an appearance that justice is for sale and that a judge's decision may be influenced by a financial incentive or disincentive rather than by the law and the facts. Even if a judge is completely fair, the appearance of impropriety harms the integrity and reputation of the judiciary when salary is connected to the outcome of cases.

3. An en banc hearing is a hearing in which all of the judges of a particular court hear a case jointly in order to reach a binding, and hopefully, uniform decision. The three criminal court judges were requested to conduct an en banc hearing in this case so that all three courts in the county would ultimately apply the same ruling, although as it turned out, the three judges did not agree on the result.

4. When judges and government officials emphasize the fee-generating aspects of the judicial system, public trust and confidence in the courts is undermined. Similarly, when judges are praised or rewarded for their success in raising funds through fines and court costs, rather than for the judicious performance of their duties, the public may become cynical about the courts and disrespect judicial decisions.

5. New courts and judgeships are created by legislatures.

6. The legislature is prohibited from reducing a judge's salary or eliminating a judge's position during a term in office in order to prevent the legislature from interfering with judicial independence and from intimidating or retaliating against a judge.

7. This case illustrates the importance of reviewing state constitutions. Sometimes, state constitutions contain unique provisions that may provide a basis for argument in a case.

Chapter XV
Gilbert v. Richardson, 452 S.E.2d 476 (Ga.),
reconsideration denied, (Ga. 1994)

1. What is immunity?

2. What is the difference between absolute and qualified immunity?

3. What is the doctrine of "sovereign immunity?"

4. What is the purpose of the doctrine of sovereign immunity?

5. Why would a state waive sovereign immunity and allow suits against government entities?

6. What does it mean to be "liable?"

7. What is the doctrine of "official immunity?"

CHAPTER XV

GILBERT v. RICHARDSON
452 S.E. 2d 476 (Ga.), *reconsideration denied,* (Ga. 1994)

For many years during my practice, I worked on cases with William Ralph Hill, Jr., a now-retired Superior Court Judge serving the Lookout Mountain Judicial Circuit in Northwest Georgia. Together, we tried and handled several criminal cases as well as a case involving a tractor trailer accident that, at the time, yielded the highest settlement amount in that area in a case of its kind. Ralph and I also were involved in the case of *Gilbert v. Richardson*, 452 S.E.2d 476 (Ga. 1994), a landmark decision of the Georgia Supreme Court involving the doctrines of sovereign and official immunity.

The Gilberts sued Walker County, the Walker County Sheriff Albert Millard, and Deputy Sheriff Kathy Richardson when Richardson collided with their car while she was responding to an emergency call. The Gilberts claimed that Richardson was driving negligently and carelessly when the accident occurred and that since she was on duty, the county and the department were liable as her employers under the doctrine of respondeat superior.

Both Millard and Richardson sought to have the case against them dismissed on legal grounds. Sheriff Millard argued that he was entitled to absolutely immune from suit under the doctrine of sovereign immunity and Deputy Richardson argued that she was entitled to immunity under the doctrine of official immunity. The trial judge, the Honorable John B. Wood, agreed with the defendants and dismissed the case against them. The Georgia Court of Appeals affirmed the decision of the trial court in *Gilbert v. Richardson*, 440 S.E. 2d 684 (Ga. Ct. App. 1994). But the Georgia Supreme Court accepted the case and issued a decision that remains controlling law on these issues.

Georgia, like most states, had long honored the doctrine of sovereign immunity protecting the government from being sued without its consent. The state retained immunity until an amendment to the

Georgia Constitution was passed providing that the state, its departments, and agencies waived immunity "in actions for which liability
insurance protection was provided." Ga. Const. of 1983, Art. 1, §2, ¶
IX. Following the constitutional amendment and a statutory enact-
ment, sovereign immunity was extended to the state, its departments,
and agencies except as waived by act of the Georgia General Assembly. The Georgia Supreme Court had interpreted the Georgia law to
extend sovereign immunity to counties. *Toombs County v. O'Neal*, 330
S.E.2d 95 (Ga. 1985).

On behalf of the Gilberts, we argued that sovereign immunity
was waived as a result of a Georgia statute providing for waiver "to the
extent of the amount of liability insurance [purchased by a county] for
the negligence of its officers, agents, servants, attorneys, or employees
arising from the use of a motor vehicle." *Gilbert v. Richardson*, 452
S.E.2d 476, 480 (Ga. 1994) (citing O.C.G.A. §33-24-51). Because the
county had purchased liability insurance, the county had waived sovereign immunity to the extent of the amount of the liability insurance
policy. The Georgia Supreme Court agreed with us that Sheriff Millard, who was sued in his capacity as county sheriff, stood in the shoes
of the county, with sovereign immunity being waived to the extent of
the county's liability insurance policy.

Georgia also recognized the doctrine of official immunity, which
provided limited protection from suit for government officers and
employees who were performing official duties. Under Georgia law,
officers and employees could only be sued when they negligently performed or failed to perform their "ministerial functions" or when they
caused harm while performing "official functions" with "actual malice
or with actual intent to cause injury." *Id.* at 483. In *Gilbert*, the Georgia
Supreme Court decided that the term "official functions" included any
act performed in the scope of the government officer or employees'
duties. *Id.* Because Deputy Sheriff Richardson was acting within her
official duties in responding to an emergency call, she was entitled to
official immunity.

Since Sheriff Millard was sued under the theory of respondeat
superior, alleging that he was liable as the employer of Deputy Sheriff
Richardson, he argued that he, too, was entitled to protection under

the doctrine of official immunity. But the Georgia Supreme Court saw things differently. Sheriff Millard could not claim the benefit of Deputy Sheriff Richardson's official immunity because "official immunity of a public employee does not protect a government entity from liability under the doctrine of respondeat superior... . Since deputy sheriffs are employed by the sheriff rather than the county, sheriffs may be liable in their official capacity for a deputy's negligence in performing an official function." *Id.* at 484.

Thus, although Deputy Sheriff Richardson was immune from liability, the sheriff remained liable up to the extent of the county's liability insurance coverage. The case against Walker County was sent back to the trial court and eventually was settled.

What I Know

1. Immunity generally means that a party cannot be sued without their permission, but in practical terms, a party who is entitled to immunity may be sued, but the lawsuit will be dismissed based on their immunity. The term is most usually a part of the phrase "sovereign immunity" discussed in 4 *infra.*

2. Absolute immunity is a type of immunity that confers complete immunity from suits for damages confers complete immunity from suits for damages for individuals who were acting within the scope of their official duties.

3. Sovereign immunity is a principle derived from the English common law based on the principle that the King could do no wrong. Sovereign immunity in the United States refers to the fact that state and federal governments may not be sued without their consent. Sovereign immunity can be waived as, for example, when the state or federal government passes statutes that allow individuals to sue the government in certain kinds of cases.

4. The purpose of the sovereign immunity doctrine is to free the government from frequent exposure to litigation in order to allow government actors to perform their official duties without constant concern about being sued. Additionally, immunity allows government to avoid the waste of time, energy, and resources involved in defending lawsuits and allows individuals to serve the government without fear of personal liability for their acts or the acts of their subordinates.

5. A state may waive sovereign immunity in order to give its citizens some recourse in the courts when they are wronged by government actors.

6. To be "liable" means that a person is accountable for damages caused by their actions.

7. While the state and federal governments are immunized by sovereign immunity, public officials enjoy official immunity from personal liability when they are acting in the course and scope of their official duties.

Chapter XVI
State v. Whaley, 982 S.W.2d 346 (Tenn. 1997)

1. How does a jurisdiction's sentencing philosophy impact punishment?

2. How does the frequency and occurrence of crime impact punishment?

3. What is meant by the phrase a "repeat offender?" What does "recidivist" mean?

4. What are sentencing factors?

5. What sentencing factors should enhance (or increase) or mitigate (or reduce) a sentence?

6. What does it mean for a conviction to be "invalid on its face?"

7. How does an attorney use a case or argument as an effective tool in plea negotiations?

CHAPTER XVI

STATE v. WHALEY
982 S.W. 2d 346 (Tenn. 1997)

Sentencing guidelines generally authorize courts to give repeat offenders higher sentences than first offenders. A sentence may be enhanced by an individual's prior conviction, even where the prior conviction occurred in a different state. For example, when an individual charged with driving under the influence of an intoxicant (DUI) has a prior conviction for DUI in a foreign state within ten years of the date of their new arrest (or, perhaps, conviction), the individual will face a significantly enhanced sentence, including an increase in the jail sentence, the amount of the fine, and the length of the mandatory minimum period of incarceration.

Because DUI statutes vary, lawyers can sometimes argue that the out-of-state conviction is so dissimilar as to not constitute a prior conviction in Tennessee. This is one of the arguments that I raised in the case of *State v. Whaley*, 982 S.W.2d 346 (Tenn. 1997).

Defendant Whaley had been charged with several DUI offenses in Georgia. When she was tried on her Tennessee charge, the jury convicted her as a second offender. I raised three challenges to the enhanced sentence. First, I challenged the use of a Georgia conviction to enhance her sentence because of its dissimilarity from the Tennessee offense. Second, I challenged the vagueness and overbreadth of the Tennessee DUI statute, which by not requiring similarity of prior convictions allowed "creative and discriminatory use of the statute." I also challenged the validity of a Georgia conviction. The trial court disagreed with my arguments and sentenced my client as a second offender to eleven months and twenty-nine days (11-29), but announced that he might consider a suspended sentence after service of one hundred twenty (120) days.

On appeal, the Tennessee Court of Criminal Appeals upheld the denial of the statutory challenges. However, the certified copy of the

Georgia conviction that had been stipulated did not bear a judge's signature; nor did it indicate whether Whaley was represented by counsel or waived her right to counsel. Therefore, the prior Georgia conviction was "invalid on its face" and could not be used to establish her status as s second offender based on *State v. McClintock*, 732 S.W.2d 268 (Tenn.1987), a decision of the Tennessee Supreme Court holding that a "facially invalid judgment could not be used to enhance punishment in a subsequent prosecution." *State v. McClintock*, 732 S.W.2d at 272.

The appellate court remanded the case to the trial court for resentencing as a first offender and as a result we were able to negotiate a minimum sentence. The Tennessee Supreme Court has not fully resolved whether Tennessee DUI's enhancement statute requires that foreign convictions be based on similar DUI provisions and thus, this issue should continue to be pressed in DUI cases. The *Whaley* decision may also be a useful tool in DUI plea negotiations.

What I Know

1. There are five distinct sentencing philosophies: retribution, incapacitation, deterrence, restoration, and rehabilitation. States use a variety and combination of philosophies in formulating their sentencing laws. When a state emphasizes protection of society as its sentencing goal, it will likely endorse sentences that require retribution, incapacitation, and deterrence and convicted defendants will more likely be incarcerated. In contrast, in a jurisdiction with sentencing philosophies that favor restoration and rehabilitation, punishment will focus on education, training, treatment for addictions and mental health issues, and other means of helping offenders become contributing and productive members of society. These jurisdictions are more likely to offer probationary sentences in lieu of incarceration.

2. The frequency and occurrence of crime impact individual sentences as well as sentencing practices. Generally, individual offenders who re-offend will be punished more harshly. When community recidivism rates are high, the prosecution may seek and the judge may deliver harsher sentences in order to send a message that deters criminal activity.

3. A repeat offender, also known as a recidivist, is someone who re-offends. Recidivism refers to the tendency of individuals to reoffend.

4. Judges consider sentencing factors to determine an appropriate sentence in each situation. Common sentencing factors include: age, education level, social and mental history, intellect, past criminal record, the nature of the crime, the circumstances under which the crime was committed, the status of the victim, and the remorse expressed by the offender.

5.   Enhancement factors are those that lead the judge to sentence an offender more harshly, while mitigating factors are those that lead the judge to sentence an offender more leniently.

6. A conviction is "invalid on its face" when it can be determined simply by looking at the legal documents that set out the conviction that the conviction is void. In this case, because the legal documents representing the Georgia convictions did not show that Whaley had waived her right to counsel, the conviction was invalid on its face and, therefore, void.

7. When counsel is negotiating a plea agreement in a case, counsel researches the law and facts in order to develop legal and factual arguments that support counsel's position on an issue or that weakens opposing counsel's position on an issue. Each side's perspective of the strengths and weaknesses of its case, based on the facts and the law, are significant factors in plea negotiations.

Chapter XVII
State v. Downey, 945 S.W.2d 102 (Tenn. 1997)

1. What is a case of "first impression?"

2. What is the interplay between public policy and law?

3. How does the use of roadblocks or checkpoints advance the goals of the criminal legal system?

4. How does the use of roadblocks or checkpoints impact the rights of individuals?

5. What are the advantages and disadvantages of granting discretion to an individual, such as a police officer, in the criminal legal system?

6. What is the interplay between provisions of the federal and state constitutions?

7. What does it mean for a state court to rule on an issue based on "independent state grounds?"

CHAPTER XVII

STATE v. DOWNEY
945 S.W.2d 102 (Tenn.1997)

This was a case of first impression in Tennessee, addressing whether the police can establish a roadblock to stop and question motorists whose conduct has been unremarkable and free from any suspicion. The argument against random roadblocks was based on guarantees under both the United States and Tennessee Constitutions providing that police may not conduct "unreasonable" searches and seizures. U.S. Const. amend. IV; Tenn. Const. Article I, Section 7.[1]

On August 8, 1992, at approximately midnight, Lieutenant (Lt.) Ronnie Hill of the Tennessee Highway Patrol and numerous members of the Chattanooga Police Department Driving under the Influence (DUI) Task Force, as well as auxiliary members of the Hamilton County Sheriff's Department, set up a roadblock on Hixson Pike in Hamilton County, Tennessee. Lt. Hill testified that he had chosen the site for the roadblock without obtaining his supervising officer's approval regarding the establishment, time, or location of the roadblock. Similarly, Lt. Hill did not provide any "advance public announcement of the existence, time or location of the roadblock." *State v. Downey*, 945 S.W.2d 102,105 (Tenn. 1997).

Lt. Hill testified that he supervised the operations of the roadblock, including instructing other officers at the scene. During the roadblock, four to six patrol cars, with blue lights on, were positioned on both sides and in the center turn lane of Hixson Pike. The participating officers did not have discretion as to which cars to stop; rather, they stopped every car.

---

1 The Fourth Amendment to the United States Constitution provides that "[t]he right of the people to be secure in their persons, houses, papers, and effects, against unreasonable searches and seizures, shall not be violated. . . ." U.S. Const. amend. IV. Article I, Section 7 of the Tennessee Constitution, similarly provides "that the people shall be secure in their persons, houses, papers, and possessions, from unreasonable searches and seizures. . . ."

When Downey was stopped at the roadblock, she was asked to pull to the side of the road to perform field sobriety tests because Hamilton County Deputy Sheriff Robert Stames, a member of the DUI Task Force, said he smelled alcohol on her breath. After Downey allegedly failed the tests, she was arrested.

In my representation of Downey, I challenged her stop and her arrest under the state and federal constitutional provisions prohibiting unreasonable searches and seizures. Although Lt. Hill attempted to portray the roadblock as a routine drivers' license checkpoint conducted under the authority of written guidelines established by the Tennessee Department of Safety, we argued in our motion to suppress the evidence that the so-called drivers' license checkpoint was merely a "subterfuge" to arrest drunken drivers. *Id.* at 111. This argument was overruled by the trial court and the appellate courts, but for other reasons, we were successful in the end.

Following a lengthy analysis of state decisions and approaches, the Tennessee Supreme Court held that the use of roadblocks to detect drunken drivers was not a per se constitutional violation under either the state or federal constitution. The court relied upon the United States Supreme Court's decision in *Michigan v. Sitz*, 496 U.S. 444 (1990), for its determination that roadblocks and checkpoints are not per se violations of the federal constitution. To determine the reasonableness of a roadblock "seizure," which is less intrusive than a full arrest, a court must balance "the gravity of the public concerns served by the seizure, the degree to which the seizure advances the public interest, and the severity of the interference with individual liberty." *State v. Downey*, 945 S.W.2d at 107 (citing *Michigan v. Sitz*, 496 U.S. at 453 & 455 (quoting *Brown v. Texas*, 443 U.S. 447, 450-51 (1979)).

Interestingly, although the United States Supreme Court ruled that checkpoints were not per se violations of the Fourth Amendment in *Sitz*, the Michigan Supreme Court, based on independent state grounds, held that such checkpoints were per se violations of the Michigan Constitution. *Sitz v. Department of State Police*, 506 N.W.2d 209 (Mich. 1993). Unfortunately, the Tennessee Supreme Court in *Downey* did not follow Michigan's lead, choosing instead to adopt the balancing approach. The Tennessee Supreme Court endorsed the use of sobriety checkpoints when "established and operated in accordance with predetermined operational guidelines and supervisory authority that minimize the risk of arbitrary intrusion on individuals and limit the discretion of law enforcement officers at the scene." *State v. Downey*, 945 S.W.2d at 104. The Hixson Pike roadblock was not conducted in accordance with those restrictions and, thus, resulted in unreasonable and unconstitutional seizures.

In opposition to this author's opinion, the Tennessee Supreme Court declined to conclude that the roadblock was a subterfuge, although it noted that much of the evidence suggested that the "actual purpose" of the roadblock was "the detection of alcohol-impaired motorists." *Id.* at 111. In this author's opinion, sobriety roadblocks are mere subterfuges, set up to facilitate easy arrests in order to secure substantial grants given by the National Highway Traffic Safety Administration (NHTSA) for the enforcement of DUI laws.[2]

At the time of the Hixson Pike roadblock, the Tennessee Highway Patrol had not adopted General Order 410, addressing officers' discretion at driver's license checkpoints. After the *Downey* case, General Order 410 was adopted, and later amended to address sobriety checkpoints, providing a source of litigation on several issues including the failure to give advance public notice of roadblocks, as discussed in Chapter 24 *infra*, reviewing the case of *State v. Franklin*, 2018 WL 3998766 (Tenn. Crim. App. Aug. 21, 2018). Many officers have told me privately that given the difficulties of complying with General Order 410's guidelines for establishing a legally compliant sobriety checkpoint, checkpoints are a less effective deterrent against driving under the influence than normal traffic patrol.

---

2 NHTSA's funding is discussed on the webpage for the United States Department of Transportation at www.transportation.gov.

What I Know

1. A "case of first impression" is a case that raises a legal issue that has not been previously decided by a controlling court. Lower courts may have issued conflicting opinions on the issue prompting the appellate court, whose decisions control those of the lower courts, to review the case of first impression in order to resolve the issue and facilitate uniformity of decision among lower courts.

2. Officials in the executive and legislative branches effectuate public policy through executive orders and agendas and legislative actions. The democratic theory is that the elected officials are elected based on their platforms, which they then carry into office and effectuate through laws, executive orders, and government policies.

3. If, as here, the legislature adopts a public policy of strictly enforcing DUI laws and vigorously punishing DUI offenders, roadblocks can be a mechanism used to advance this policy. When police set up roadblocks and stop every car, police have an opportunity to observe every driver and in doing so can take appropriate measures against those who are driving under the influence. The use of roadblocks also has a deterrent effect because motorists presumably will be motivated to not drink and drive in order to avoid being arrested if stopped at a roadblock

4. The use of roadblocks or sobriety checkpoints implicate the Fourth Amendment's protection against unreasonable searches and seizures because when a driver is stopped at a roadblock, the driver is "seized," at least temporarily. By seizing the individual, the police have interfered with the individual's freedom of movement. Before an individual can be seized, the Fourth Amendment generally requires that the police have some individualized reasonable cause, but when all drivers are stopped at a roadblock, without any basis for believing that the

drivers are violating the law, the stop and resulting seizure is without individualized reasonable cause.

5. The advantage of allowing police officer discretion is that a fair and competent officer can then exercise well-reasoned judgment to act properly in light of the circumstances; the disadvantage, of course, is that some officers who are given discretion will not act reasonably but will abuse their discretion and exercise their authority in an unfair, discriminatory, or inappropriate manner.

6. The United States Constitution applies to and restricts the federal government. The United States Supreme Court has interpreted certain of the first ten amendments, the Bill of Rights, to be "incorporated" by the Due Process Clause of the Fourteenth Amendment, so as to make those incorporated provisions applicable to the states. In those circumstances, in which the federal constitution applies in the states, the states must follow the requirements of the federal constitution or offer their citizens greater rights. State constitutional provisions often mirror those of the federal constitution, but state courts may interpret their own constitutions more broadly. In any event, state constitutions limit and restrict the actions of state government.

7. When a state court rules on "independent state grounds" that means that the state court is basing its decision on a provision of state law, rather than a provision of the federal constitution. States may not render decisions that undermine the protections of the federal constitution, but they may, based on independent state grounds, protect their citizens more broadly by granting greater rights than those recognized by the United States Constitution.

Chapter XVIII
State v. Binette, 33 S.W.3d 215 (Tenn. 2000)

1. What is a motion to suppress?

2. What constitutional rights are protected by allowing a defendant to file a motion to suppress evidence secured from an unlawful stop?

3. What public safety concerns are undermined when a motion to suppress evidence based on an unlawful stop is granted?

4. What happens when a motion to suppress evidence secured from an unlawful stop is granted?

5. Why does the law require a police officer to have a legitimate reason to stop a vehicle?

6. What is meant by reasonable suspicion supported by specific and articulable facts?

7. What is a conditional guilty plea?

CHAPTER XVIII

STATE V. BINETTE
33 S.W.3d 215 (Tenn. 2000)

Officer Gary Davis, Chattanooga Police Department DUI Task Force, stopped Gary Binette after observing his driving and charged with driving under the influence (DUI). Jerry Sloan, then an attorney in private practice, represented Binette. By filing a motion to suppress evidence, Attorney Sloan challenged the stop and subsequent arrest as invalid, arguing that Officer Davis had no lawful basis to stop Binette. In determining whether to grant the motion to suppress, the trial judge relied completely on a review of the video recorded in Officer Davis' vehicle and the officer's comments describing the defendant's driving.[1]

After viewing the video and Officer Davis' accompanying comments, the trial court denied the motion, but allowed the defendant to enter a "conditional guilty plea," reserving the right to appeal the issue of whether the stop was lawful. The Tennessee Court of Criminal Appeals affirmed the trial judge's decision denying the motion to suppress and the defendant sought review in the Tennessee Supreme Court. This is the point at which I became involved as amicus curiae filing a brief on behalf of my then-law firm, Summers and Wyatt (now Summers, Rufolo, and Rodgers).

The Tennessee Supreme Court framed the legal issue on appeal as "whether reasonable suspicion, based on specific and articulable facts, existed to authorize a stop of the defendant's vehicle." *State v. Binette*, 33 S.W.2d 215, 216 (Tenn. 2000). In analyzing the legal issue, the Supreme Court reviewed the video and Officer Davis' comments; concluded that the evidence did not support a "finding that the police officer acted with reasonable suspicion when he stopped the defen-

---

1 Officer Davis did not testify as he had resigned from the Chattanooga's Police Department at the time of the hearing.

dant;" and dismissed the charges against the defendant. *Id.*

In reversing the trial judge's ruling, the Supreme Court empha-sized that it was required to examine the trial record de novo, mean-ing "anew." Since the trial judge was simply viewing the video, and not judging the credibility of testifying witnesses, the appellate court was "just as capable to review the evidence and draw their own conclu-sions." *Id.* at 217.

In order for the stop to be valid, "at the time that Officer Davis turned on his vehicle's blue lights, he must have had reasonable sus-picion, supported by specific and articulable facts, that Binette had committed, or was about to commit, a criminal offense." *Id.* at 218. Although Davis' commentary on the video indicated that the defen-dant was repeatedly crossing the center line, making a hard swerve, and speeding, the Court found these statements to be "clearly con-tradicted by the visual portion of the tape." *Id.* at 219. Although the defendant's car may have touched the center lane, touching without crossing over the lane did not constitute a reasonable suspicion to stop the defendant's car.

What I Know

1. A motion to suppress evidence is a motion filed by the accused that requests that certain evidence be excluded because the evidence was illegally obtained.

2. A motion to suppress protects an individual's constitutional rights. For example, a motion to suppress based on the Fourth Amendment challenges the infringement of an individual's right to be free from "unreasonable searches and seizures," while a motion to suppress under the Fifth Amendment protects a person's right to be free from self-incrimination. Similarly, a motion to suppress may raise an individual's right to counsel and challenge, for example, a police interrogation during which the accused was not advised of the right to counsel. In addition to challenging the admission of tangible evidence and an accused's statements, motions to suppress may also be filed to challenge police identification procedures that are "unnecessarily suggestive."

3. When a motion to suppress evidence is granted, the prosecution cannot admit the excluded evidence or rely upon the excluded evidence in its case-in-chief at trial. In some circumstances, when the suppressed evidence is critical to the case, the charges will be dismissed or reduced. Because the public has an interest in the enforcement of criminal laws and the apprehension of those engaging in criminal conduct, it is essential that officers engage in police practices that are consistent with the constitutional rights of the accused.

4. The granting of a motion to suppress can lead to the dismissal of a case when the excluded evidence is vital and the case against the accused cannot be made without the evidence. If the excluded evidence is not critical to the case, the prosecution will proceed, but without the admission of or reference to the excluded evidence.

5. The law requires an officer to have a legitimate reason to stop a vehicle because individuals have a right to privacy, which includes the right to go about their business without interference unless they are violating the law. If an officer stops a vehicle without a legitimate reason, the stop is unreasonable and, in most circumstances, violates the Fourth Amendment.

6. "Reasonable suspicion supported by specific and articulable facts" exists when an officer has some identifiable facts that lead the officer to reasonably conclude that an individual is committing or about to commit a crime. The standard requires more than a mere "hunch."

7. A conditional guilty plea is a type of guilty plea that allows the accused to enter the plea, subject to the appeal of a contested and controlling legal issue. In the event the appellate court rules in the accused's favor on the contested legal issue, the accused is allowed to withdraw the guilty plea. For example, in this case, the accused entered a conditional guilty plea, but reserved the question of whether the traffic stop was legal: if the traffic stop was determined to be legal, the accused's case would be returned to the trial court for sentencing, but if the traffic stop was determined to be illegal, the accused's guilty plea would be set aside. Because the legality of the stop was a dispositive legal issue in the case, the conditional guilty plea was an efficient mechanism for deciding the case because it enabled the legal issue to be resolved by the appellate court without a trial of the case.

Chapter XIX
City of Chattanooga v. Davis, 54 S.W.3d 248 (Tenn. 2001)

1. What do you think motivated the framers of the Tennessee Constitution to include the unique provisions found in Article VI, Section 14, requiring that fines in excess of fifty dollars ($50) be assessed by a jury?

2. Why are some forms of conduct punishable by both city ordinances and state laws?

3. What is the difference between a punitive and non-punitive assessment?

4. Why are punitive assessments considered "fines" and protected by the right to jury trial in Article VI, Section 14 of the Tennessee Constitution, while non-punitive assessments are not?

5. What was the likely motivation for the Chattanooga police directive that required police officers to cite individuals for city ordinance violations, rather than for state statute violations, when the accused's conduct violated both?

6. Why was the police directive likely of concern to members of the Tennessee Supreme Court?

CHAPTER XIX

CITY OF CHATTANOOGA v. DAVIS
54 S.W. 3d 248 (Tenn. 2001)

Like the circumstances that gave rise to *State v. Freeman,* discussed in Chapter XIV, this case also grew out of a city judge's unconstitutional practice of assessing fines in excess fifty dollars ($50) dollars without a jury[1] in violation of Article VI, Section 14 of the Tennessee Constitution.

On December 6, 1998, a Chattanooga City police officer cited Kevin Davis for violating a provision of the Chattanooga City Code prohibiting driving "any vehicle in willful or wanton disregard for the safety of persons or property."[2] Davis appeared in court without a lawyer. He was not informed of his right to counsel or his right to a jury trial. Davis plead guilty and was fined three hundred dollars ($300).

Unsatisfied with his treatment by the court at his hearing, Davis hired our office. We appealed the conviction to the Hamilton County Criminal Court and requested dismissal of the charges based on the violation of two provisions of the Tennessee Constitution,[3] including Article VI, Section 14's provision entitling Davis to a jury trial in all cases in which a fine in excess of fifty dollars ($50) was imposed. The Hamilton County Criminal Court agreed that the Chattanooga City Court's imposition of a three hundred dollar ($300) fine violated Article VI, Section 14 of the Tennessee Constitution and reduced the fine to fifty dollars ($50); a few weeks later, the criminal court judge entered an order enjoining the city of Chattanooga from imposing monetary penalties in excess of fifty dollars ($50).

---

1 City courts in Tennessee do not have jurisdiction to empanel a jury.

2 Chattanooga City Code Section 24-13(a)

3 We also challenged the provisions of Tennessee Code Annotated Section 6-54-306, as violating the Equal Protection Clause and the Class Legislation Clause of Article XI, Section 8 of the Tennessee Constitution. Although we were successful on this challenge in in the trial court, the Tennessee Supreme Court did not reference the provision in its recitation of the procedural history of the case. *City of Chattanooga v. Davis,* 54 S.W.3d 248 (Tenn. 2001).

The city of Chattanooga requested that the criminal court dissolve or modify the order; additionally, the Tennessee Attorney General's office became involved in order to defend the constitutionality of the statutes. Following two days of hearings, the Hamilton County Criminal Court ruled in Davis' favor finding that because David did not waive his right to trial by jury, he could not be fined in excess of fifty dollars ($50). The criminal court also ruled in our favor on other grounds, finding two statutory provisions and one city code section to be in violation of provisions of the Tennessee Constitution and state law.

The city of Chattanooga sought and was granted an extraordinary appeal in the Tennessee Court of Appeals. Feeling constrained by prior precedent, that court reversed the rulings of the lower court and dissolved the injunction, reasoning that under prior decisions, the assessments imposed could not be considered "fines" within the meaning of Article VI, Section 14, of the Tennessee Constitution. *City of Chattanooga v Davis*, 2000 WL 1635604, *6-8 (Tenn. Ct. App. Oct. 31, 2000). Judge Herschel P. Franks dissented. On Davis' behalf, we sought and were granted permission to appeal to the Tennessee Supreme Court.[4]

Writing for the five-judge majority, Justice William M. Barker detailed the uniqueness of Article VI, Section 14, noting that the provision "is unique in the whole of American constitutional law, and no other provision like it may be found either in the Federal Constitution or in any other modern state constitution." *City of Chattanooga v. Davis*, 54 S.W.3d 248, 257 (Tenn. 2001). The history of the provision, though sparse, suggested that its intent "was to prevent judges from imposing unreasonable fines, and to prevent confiscation of the citizen's substance under the guise of a statute applied by a judicial tribunal." *Id.* at 258 (citing *Upchurch v. State*, 281 S.W. 462, 464 (1926); *State v. Martin*, 940 S.W.2d 567, 570 (Tenn.1997)). History made it equally clear that the constitutional provision only applied to punitive assessments and did not bar "the imposition of non-punitive measures." *Id.* at 259.

---

4 Because a case arising in Davidson County raised the same issues, *see Barrett v. Metropolitan Government of Nashville & Davidson Co.*, 2000 WL 798657 (Tenn. Ct. App., June 22, 2000), the Tennessee Supreme Court granted permission to appeal and issued decisions in both cases.

In his excellent opinion, Justice Barker unraveled prior decisions that turned merely on the wording used in an ordinance, used legal logic, and expressively referenced Shakespeare to reach the conclusion that the purpose of the fine imposed on Davis for reckless driving was punitive.

> First, and without question, the precise name given to the sanction is hardly determinative of its substantive purpose or effect, and this method of constitutional interpretation is simply inadequate to properly resolve the question before us today. As the Bard of 'Avon classically and eloquently expressed the sentiment, "What's in a name? That which we call a rose, By any other name would smell as sweet." *Romeo and Juliet*, act II, scene ii. Indeed, if one needed only to change the appellation of a constitutional protection in order to avoid its use as a shield against the power of the State, one could scarcely imagine that any safeguard of liberty would be worth its recitation in a written constitution.

Id. at 260. The test the court applied to determine whether the assessment was punitive, and thus, a fine, was "whether the pecuniary sanction was imposed to serve primarily as a punitive measure." *Id.* at 265.

Justice Barker also expressed concern about a policy adopted by the Chattanooga Chief of Police to be followed by officers of the department.[5] The policy directed officers who issued traffic citations for violations for which "there is both a state and city violation, ... to cite the person for violation of the city ordinance. The issuance of citations to General Sessions Court is to be used only for charges in which a city ordinance does not exist." *Id.* at 279.

---

5 In a footnote, Justice Barker referenced comments made to the city council by a city judge who was requesting a pay raise based on his increasing city revenues to over one million dollars ($1,000,000) with practices including imposing fines in excess of fifty dollars ($50): "Also, at this meeting, the city court judge remarked that 'if persons are fined for driving without a license[,] we keep the entire amount[,] plus a part of the court costs; that money has been redirected back into the City of Chattanooga.'" The city judge suggested that the redirecting of money was one reason that the revenue numbers from the city court "are as impressive as they are." *City of Chattanooga v. Davis*, 54 S.W.3d at 280 n. 27. The judge who requested, and received, the pay raise during his term of office, as prohibited by the Tennessee Constitution, would eventually return to private practice.

In many respects, this practice by the City of Chattanooga perhaps represents the most disturbing aspect of this case. A letter from the District Attorney General to the Chief of Police contained in the record summarizes the problem in clear and unequivocal terms: "Your directive has the potential for allowing state law violators to avoid appropriate punishment, removes my ability to enhance punishment for state law violator[s], and infringes upon my constitutional duty and responsibility to prosecute those who violate the laws of the State of Tennessee." Indeed, through this "potential" infringement, the City of Chattanooga has received a financial windfall, which, according to the city court judge himself, was a direct result of the City Council passing ordinances that transferred state cases to city court, "thereby allowing the revenues to remain in Chattanooga."

Although we had established a compelling case showing that city policies and practices were infringing upon the District Attorney General's constitutional and statutory authority, the Tennessee Supreme Court, nonetheless, declined to decide the issue, because they believed we had failed to demonstrate any actual harm resulting from the unlawful practices alleged. Whether by coincidence or otherwise, the District Attorney General removed all state cases from city court and transferred them to the Hamilton County General Sessions Court as described in the case of *State v. Freeman*, Chapter XIV, *supra*. This transformed the City Court of Chattanooga into a court that dealt almost exclusively with traffic tickets, with its jurisdiction for fines limited, as the Tennessee Constitution requires, to fifty dollars ($50).

What I Know

1. The framers of the Tennessee Constitution likely prohibited judges from assessing fines over fifty dollars ($50) to protect citizens from unreasonable fines and to diminish the unfettered power of the judiciary.

2. Some conduct is punishable under both city and state law because the state legislature has allowed the city to prosecute such offenses. Since law enforcement functions are performed by a range of offices – municipal, county, and state – overlapping statutes make the process more efficient.

3. A punitive assessment is designed to punish conduct. A non-punitive assessment is designed to remedy damaging conduct.

4. Punitive assessments are considered "fines" because they are not a remedial method of making a damaged party whole again. They are, instead, payments to the government to punish past conduct and deter the same conduct in the future. Non-punitive assessments are not fines for the opposite reason: their entire purpose is to make a damaged party whole.

5. The motivation behind the Chattanooga police directive was to raise funds for the city of Chattanooga. The city retained the money from the payment of fines.

6. The Tennessee Supreme Court was likely concerned about the police directive because of the potential incentive the directive could create. Officers could be incentivized to issue excessive tickets and courts could be incentivized to routinely impose maximum fines in order to raise revenue for the city and assure their own positions and salaries. In this manner, the directive has the potential to give the city judge an interest in the outcome of cases, which is counter to the idea of a fair, neutral, and independent judiciary.

Chapter XX
State v. Hicks, 55 S.W.3d 515 (Tenn. 2001)

1. How does this case illustrate how courts use precedent?

2. What does it mean to try to factually distinguish a case in order to avoid the application of precedent?

3. What role does the goal of public safety play in the administration of justice?

4. How does a roadblock further the goals of public safety?

5. How does a roadblock interfere with individual rights?

6. How do the courts balance the conflict between the goals of public safety and the rights of individuals?

7. What does "compelling state interest" mean?

8. What is the interplay between an agency's departmental policy and state and federal law?

9. How does this case demonstrate the use of policy to challenge law enforcement practices?

10. How does this case demonstrate the use of policy and fact-based research to supplement legal research?

CHAPTER XX

STATE v. HICKS
55 S.W. 3d 515 (Tenn. 2001)

In this case, we challenged the constitutionality of drivers' license roadblocks. As a result of our work in *State v. Downey*, 945 S.W.2d 102 (Tenn. 1997) (challenging constitutionality of sobriety checkpoints), *see* Chapter XVII *supra*, we were very familiar with the requirements of General Order 410 issued by the Tennessee Department of Safety and had used it to challenge police conduct that deviated from the guidelines. The roadblock in this case, occurring near the Hamilton County and Marion County line, was established pursuant to General Order 410, but as was true in *Downey* and other cases, compliance with the requirements of the order was incomplete. The six officers involved in the roadblock were from the Tennessee Highway Patrol (THP), the Chattanooga Police Department, and the Red Bank Police Department ((a municipality that adjoins the city limits of Chattanooga) and included a K-9 officer and an officer carrying a photo of a suspect known to police as the "North Chattanooga Rapist."

On October 11, 1997, at about 1:15 a.m., Hicks was stopped by Red Bank police officer Penny and asked to produce his driver's license. A K-9 officer was summonsed when another officer indicated that he smelled marijuana. When the K-9 alerted, Hicks was arrested. When police searched his car, they found five pounds of marijuana in the passenger seat. Neither of the two THP officers was involved in Hicks' stop, search, or arrest, but THP Lieutenant (Lt.) Ronnie Hill was called to the scene during the search.

In representing Hicks, we argued that the use of a roadblock for the sole purpose of checking drivers' licenses was a violation of the state and federal constitutions because it constituted an unreasonable level of intrusion on an individual's privacy. At the hearing on the motion to suppress the evidence, Sergeant (Sgt.) Gregory Short of the Chattanooga Police Department agreed that, despite the requirements of General Order 410, the officers gave no advance notice of the road-block, posted no signs alerting motorists that they were approaching a roadblock, and did not use appropriate safety cones to direct traffic. Additionally, despite the requirements of General Order 410, none of the officers were wearing safety vests or carrying illuminated batons. Additionally, despite the requirements of a then-existing state law, officers other than THP officers stopped cars and asked for licenses.

In addition to Sgt. Short, Lt. Ronnie Hill of *Downey* fame testified and confirmed that he supervised the roadblock. As supervisor, he informed the officers that the purpose of the roadblock was to check drivers' licenses. Hill denied knowing that officers were not following the requirements of General Order 410; moreover, he said he did not request the presence of the Red Bank and Chattanooga Police Departments, did not know who did or why they were there, and did not know that they were asking questions about the so-called North Chattanooga rapist.

The trial court granted our motion to suppress, which meant that the prosecution would not be able to introduce the marijuana that was found in the car at trial as evidence against Hicks. On appeal, the State was successful in getting the Tennessee Court of Criminal Appeals to reverse the trial court, but one member of the appellate court, Judge Joe Tipton, dissented, disagreeing with the court's conclusion that drivers' license roadblocks are generally permissible under the Tennessee Constitution. *State v. Hicks*, 2000 WL 656801 (Tenn. Crim. App, May 19, 2000).

On our client's behalf, we asked the Tennessee Supreme Court to grant permission to appeal in order to resolve three issues: (1) whether drivers' license roadblocks are per se unconstitutional; (2) whether this particular roadblock was unconstitutional in light of *Downey*; and (3) whether allowing local police to stop motorists for license checks was unlawful under Tennessee statues.[1]

---

1 At the time of the roadblock, two state statutes provided that only THP officers could "stop a motor vehicle for the sole purpose of examining or checking the operator's license" or "demand the exhibition" of a driver's license unless the driver had violated some city or state law. Tenn. Code Ann. §§40-7-103(c) & 55-50-351 (a). Because the legislature had changed the law during the appeal, the Tennessee Supreme Court did not base its ruling on these laws. See 2001 Tenn. Pub. Acts ch. 700, §12 (effective July 1, 2001) (amending Tenn. Code Ann. §55-50-351 (a)).

Ultimately, we would win on the first two issues. The Tennessee Supreme Court explained:

> We cannot find a roadblock to be constitutionally reasonable unless the State first demonstrates some meaningful link between its establishment and the achievement of its compelling interest. Because the record in this case contains no such evidence, we cannot fairly conclude that the roadblock in this case meaningfully contributed to achieving the state's interest in detecting and deterring unlicensed drivers. [Even if] "there is no better way" of detecting unlicensed drivers than through roadblocks ..., we note that the lack of other effective alternatives does not alone bestow the blessing of constitutional reasonableness upon an otherwise totally ineffective roadblock. Whatever else may be said of the presence of viable alternatives, it is clear that the roadblock must promote the asserted state interest in a "sufficiently productive" fashion before it can "qualify as a reasonable law enforcement practice."

State v. Hicks, 55 S.W.3d 515, 532 (Tenn. 2001) (quoting *Delaware v. Prouse*, 440 U.S. 548, 660 (1979)). Not only had the State failed to demonstrate a sufficiently compelling state interest to justify the roadblock, the State also had failed to demonstrate that the roadblock was "sufficiently productive" and conducted in accordance within the guidelines of General Order 410. *Id.* The test previously adopted in by the court in 1997 in *Downey*, see Chapter XVII *supra*, was expressly adopted as the test for all roadblocks and checkpoints. *Id.* at 524.

Our firm has continued to press the citizen's right to privacy against unreasonable and arbitrary government intrusion. In a similar case, I worked with Tom Greenholtz, who formerly worked with our office, then became a Hamilton County Criminal Court Judge, and now is a 2022 appointee to the Tennessee Court of Criminal Appeals, to challenge the stop of our client at a sobriety checkpoint. *State v. Varner*, 160 S.W.3d 535 (Tenn. Crim. App. 2004). Although we lost our attempts to have the evidence suppressed in the trial court, we won on appeal, with the appellate court relying on *Downey and Hicks* and concluding that the officers' good-faith efforts or intentions did not serve to correct constitutional deficiencies. *State v. Varner*, 160 S.W.3d at 547-48.

The number of cases that have been favorably resolved by attacking the constitutionality of roadblocks and their failure to comport to the standards of the General Order 410[2] demonstrates how important it is for lawyers to research the law, but also to dig deeply into the underlying facts and public policies.

---

2 The violation of General Order 410 is not necessarily a constitutional violation, nor is compliance with it necessarily sufficient to satisfy the constitutional requirements. *State v. Hicks*, 55 S.W.3d 515, 535 n.11 (Tenn. 2001).

What I Know

1. In this case, counsel used the holding in *Downey*, another road-block case, to argue that because the current case was analogous, the court should rule in the same way. In other words, *Downey* was the precedent upon which counsel relied to argue for the same result in *Hicks*. Because of the principle of stare decisis, which translated means "to stand by things already decided," courts ordinarily are bound by precedent.

2. When counsel tries to factually distinguish a case to avoid the application of precedent, counsel is trying to show that the facts of the case at hand are different from the facts in the case that led to the precedent and, thus, the precedent does not apply. If the precedent does not apply, the court may reach a different result in the case at hand.

3. The government has an overarching responsibility to protect the well-being of the public. As a result, public safety concerns influence all three branches of government. When a public safety concern is identified by either the executive or legislative branch, or brought to elected officials' attention by the citizenry, the legislative branch will often attempt to tackle and remedy the problem by passing legislation, often in the form of criminal statutes. It then becomes the role of the judiciary to interpret and apply these laws in a manner that is fair and reasonable and protects the constitutional rights of the accused. Following a trial at which an accused is found guilty, a judge may be influenced by public safety concerns when imposing sentence and those same concerns may influence an appellate court reviewing the lower court's decision.

4. When motorists are required to stop at roadblocks and display proof of license and registration, the police are able to identify and

cite drivers who are not in compliance with motor vehicle or other laws. The potential for being stopped at a roadblock may also serve a deterrent function, prompting unlicensed drivers to stop driving to avoid the risk of being stopped and cited. Moreover, police officers argue that the deterrent effect of roadblocks influences other behavior, prompting drivers to be more careful when driving and to refrain from using vehicles to engage in criminal conduct.

5. Roadblocks allow the government to intrude into an individual's privacy and right to freedom of movement. At a roadblock, an individual must stop and comply with officer's requests, usually to present a driver's license and registration. Law enforcement officers argue that the intrusion into privacy is minimal for law-abiding citizens. But in some cases, based on an officer's suspicion, an individual stopped at a roadblock will be subject to further questioning which results in a further intrusion into the individual's privacy. These intrusions are magnified when the individual is unable to prepare for the situation.

6. Courts are frequently called upon to balance competing interests such as the government's interest in assuring public safety and the citizen's interest in privacy. Generally, when the government action interferes with an individual's constitutional right, the government must first establish that a compelling state interest, such as public safety, justifies its conduct and that the action it is taking achieves its goals. Then, the court must determine whether the government action unnecessarily violates individual rights. When the government action is overbroad or fails to meet its stated objectives, the citizen's constitutional rights prevail and the government action will not be tolerated.

7. A "compelling state interest" is a policy goal or interest that is so vital to the government that the government must be allowed to infringe upon individual constitutional rights in order to effectuate the goal or interest.

8. The Supremacy Clause of the United States Constitution establishes that the constitution, federal laws made pursuant to it, and treaties made under its authority, constitute the "supreme Law of the Land." U.S. Const. Art. VI, Clause 2. Thus, the federal constitution takes priority over any conflicting law. To the extent there is no conflict with

the federal constitution, a state's constitution and law constitute the primary authority for state law. The legislative and executive branch create agencies to focus on specific areas and achieve specific goals. To the extent authorized by law, these agencies create their own internal policies and rules that impact the agency's actions. These agency policies and rules may not conflict with other law or with the state or federal constitutions.

9. This case demonstrates how an agency's policy can be used in court to challenge the agency's practices when those practices are not in compliance with the stated policy. Here the Tennessee Department of Safety had adopted a policy, known as a general order that regulated how roadblocks and checkpoints were to be conducted. Counsel was able to show how the roadblock in this case failed to comply with the agency's own order. Because it was logical to assume that the department's order reflected appropriate police practices, it was appropriate for the court to consider that the agency failed to follow its own order.

10. In this case, counsel's case was likely improved by his ability to demonstrate that the Tennessee Department of Safety had adopted an order setting out requirements for roadblocks and that law enforcement officers did not follow that departmental policy when conducting the roadblock. While knowing the law and all of the underlying facts of the case is essential, discovering applicable policies and procedures can help counsel present the court with a more complete picture of the issues in the case, thus leading to a better resolution for the client.

Chapter XXI
State v. Toliver, 117 S.W.3d 216 (Tenn. 2003)

1. How does an issue that is decided by a trial judge become an appellate issue?

2. What is the interplay between issues decided at trial and issues decided on appeal?

3. What is the role of appellate courts?

4. What does it mean when a court says a party has "waived" an issue?

5. When and why do appellate courts consider issues to be waived?

6. After an appellate court finds that a trial court has made an error, why does the court conduct a separate analysis to determine whether the error harmed the accused?

7. What does it mean for an appellate court to find a trial court's error to be harmless?

8. What does it mean for an appellate court to find a trial court's error to be prejudicial or harmful error?

CHAPTER XXI

STATE v. TOLIVER
117 S.W. 3d 216 (Tenn. 2003)

Anderson Toliver was convicted of two counts of aggravated child abuse occurring on March 1 and April 9, 1998, against his step-son who was sixteen at the time the alleged incidents occurred. The charges were originally brought against Toliver and his wife in two separate indictments, one addressing the March 1 incident and the other the April 9 incident.

Toliver, a military veteran, believed in strict discipline and after marrying his new wife, (the victim's mother) he attempted to correct the bad habits of his rebellious teenage step-sons by using severe corporal punishment to discipline the victim and his younger brother whenever they received a grade below a "B." Toliver allegedly used a weight belt used to support a weightlifters back, a braided telephone cord, and a braided extension cord in the beatings.

On the morning of trial, the prosecution moved to consolidate the two indictments for trial. I objected and requested that we try the case involving the April 9 incident first. The prosecutor argued that the indictments should be consolidated because the two incidents were identical, and proof of each offense was relevant to prove the intent as to the other offense. The trial judge agreed with the State and allowed the State to proceed on both charges. After conflicting testimony by witnesses on both sides of the controversy, the jury convicted Toliver of two counts of aggravated child abuse, and he was sentenced to nine years in the Tennessee Department of Corrections.

On appeal, we raised the issue of improper consolidation, also known as joinder, but the Tennessee Court of Criminal Appeals held that the issue had been waived and could not be raised on appeal. We sought and received permission to appeal to the Tennessee Supreme Court, which did not agree that we had waived the issue. Rather the court held that the prosecution had failed to move for consolidation in advance of trial and had not established that the parties had agreed to consolidation.

In its opinion, the Tennessee Supreme Court reviewed Rules 8, 13, and 14 of the Tennessee Rules of Criminal Procedure in detail and discussed when it was proper to consolidate multiple offenses against a single defendant in a single trial. In looking meticulously at the facts in Toliver's case, the court held that the facts underlying the two charges were not so similar as to justify only one trial. The two incidents were not part of a common scheme or plan; additionally, the evidence of one offense was not relevant to any material issue in the trial of the other offense. Consolidating the two indictment for trial was an error.

Once the Tennessee Supreme Court had determined that the trial judge committed an error in consolidating the indictments for trial, the next issue was whether the error was harmful, that is whether it prejudiced the defendant or the proceeding, or whether the error could be excused as "harmless." In finding that the error prejudiced the fair trial rights of the defendant, the Tennessee Supreme Court reversed the conviction and remanded for a new trial, instructing that on re-trial no evidence of other crimes, wrongs, or acts committed against the victim or others could be admitted unless relevant to a material issue at trial.

Once again, when the case was remanded for a new trial, we were able to negotiate a settlement on reduced charges.

What I Know

1. A trial issue becomes an appellate issue when counsel objects to the issue in the trial court and then raises the issue on appeal.

2. Generally, all appellate issues were at one time trial issues, but not all trial issues become appellate issues. *See* 1 *supra*. Only when counsel makes a timely, appropriate objection in the trial court, and otherwise follows appropriate procedure to "preserve" the issue, will an appellate court review the trial court's decision.

3. The role of appellate courts is essentially to assure that trial courts correctly apply the law or, at a minimum, not egregiously misapply the law. Appellate courts may reverse trial courts when the trial court's errors are harmful, otherwise referred to as reversible errors.

4. To "waive" an issue means that counsel failed to raise an issue. Counsel can fail to raise an issue by choice, for tactical reasons, by failing to raise a timely objection, or by failing to follow appropriate objection procedure.

5. Appellate courts consider issues waived when counsel fails to object or fails to follow appropriate objection procedure. Because counsel has an obligation to give the trial judge the first opportunity to resolve any issues or correct any errors, the failure to do so results in a waiver of the issue. The waiver rule is prompted by concerns for fairness and efficiency.

6. Appellate courts separately consider whether an error harmed the accused out of concerns for finality, efficiency, and fairness. Not all errors harm the accused either because the error is inconsequential or, perhaps, because the evidence favoring the verdict reached is otherwise overwhelming. For example, when the outcome of the case would not have been different had the error not occurred, courts gen-

erally will find that the error is "harmless" and does not require that the case be retried.

7. "Harmless error" is a phrase used to indicate that the trial court's error did not prejudice the accused, undermine the reliability of the proceeding, or impact the outcome of the case.

8. "Prejudicial error" or "harmful error" is a phrase used to indicate that a trial court's errors were serious enough to require a new trial, either because the error resulted in prejudice to the accused, impacted the reliability of the proceeding, or likely impacted the outcome of the trial.

Chapter XXII
State v. Gary Wayne McCullough,
2011 WL 1378488 (Tenn. Crim. App. April 12),
perm. to oappeal denied, (Tenn. 2001)

1. What does the phrase "judge shopping" mean?

2. Why would a practice such as judge shopping offend the principle of due process and undermine fundamental fairness in the justice system?

3. What type of investigation did McCullough's lawyer have to conduct to secure necessary evidence to support the allegations of judge shopping?

4. What level of courage do you imagine a lawyer must have to question practices in the very courts in which the lawyer regularly appears?

5. It is often said that the judicial system must not only be fair, but that it also must appear to be fair. In other words, even the appearance of unfairness has a detrimental effect on the justice system. As a result, judges are required to avoid all impropriety as well as the appearance of impropriety? Why is this focus correct or incorrect?

6. How does this case illustrate how lawyers can sometimes "win" even when they lose?"

CHAPTER XXII

STATE V. McCULLOUGH
2011 WL 1378488
(Tenn. Crim. App. April 12),
perm. to appeal denied, (Tenn. 2011)

While boating on Chickamauga Lake in Hamilton County, Tennessee, Gary McCullough was arrested and charged with the offense of boating under the influence, operating a boat without lights, simple possession of marijuana, and violation of the implied consent law. McCullough was arrested by a Tennessee Wildlife Resource Agency (TWRA) officer rather than being merely given a citation.

When McCullough hired us to represent him, we investigated and learned that two of the Hamilton County General Sessions Courts seemed to hear a disproportionate number of TWRA cases. When the case was bound over and later indicted, we filed a motion to dismiss the indictment on the grounds that TWRA officers were engaged in "judge shopping" by setting their cases almost exclusively before these two judges. It was our position that the right to due process of law required that a citizen receive a fundamentally fair trial, not one where one party had purposefully selected a particular judge. Because the three Hamilton County Criminal Court judges recused themselves, the Honorable Kerry Blackwood, retired criminal court judge, who was serving as a Senior Judge, was designated by the Tennessee Supreme Court to hear the case.

During a lengthy evidentiary hearing we presented evidence from the court clerk and former Hamilton County General Sessions Judge O. Michael Carter, who had created a computer program to randomly assign cases to prevent judge shopping. When we asked for Judge Carter's comment on how one judge could be assigned five hundred and two (502) of five hundred and seven (507) cases in one year, he stated "that can't happen under the system unless someone is gaming the system." *State v. Gary Wayne McCullough,* 2011 WL 1378488,

*1 (Tenn. Crim. App. April 12, 2011). The court clerk confirmed that cases that resulted from arrests were randomly scheduled by the computer system but acknowledged that TWRA officers set their own court dates on citation cases, allowing them to schedule their cases to be heard before their judge of choice.

After hearing our evidence, Judge Blackwood held "that the anomalies in case assignments could not have been by accident or random act" and that the "TWRA officers ... had intentionally directed citation case assignments" to the two judges' courts. *Id* at 41. Judge Blackwood dismissed the indictment and sent the case back for a new preliminary hearing before a division of the general sessions court not implicated in the judge-shopping allegations. Because it was our position that the charges should be dismissed outright, we asked for and were granted an interlocutory appeal to the Tennessee Court of Criminal Appeals.

The appellate court latched on to the different scheduling mechanisms for TWRA arrest cases and TWRA citation cases. That distinction led the Tennessee Court of Criminal Appeals to vacate Judge Blackwood's dismissal and direct that the indictment against Mc-Cullough be reinstated. McCullough had been arrested, not cited, and though his case ended up before one of the judges that TWRA officers frequently chose, there was no evidence that his case assignment had been manipulated. When the case was returned to the Hamilton County Criminal Court, the court was resolved with a guilty plea on the first charge and a dismissal of the others. Additionally, corrective measures were implemented to assure that all future TWRA cases would be randomly and equally set before the five divisions of the Hamilton County General Sessions Court.

I would later learn that an additional piece of evidence might have led Judge Blackwood to dismiss the case outright. While we had established that the two judges were avid hunters and fishermen – facts that led one of the preferred judges to speculate that it was this knowledge of wildlife laws that led them to be the preferred choice for TWRA cases – both asserted that they had no control over the assignment of cases. We learned that both judges had attended a fund-raising dinner for the Tennessee chapter of the Wild Turkey Federation, at which one of the judges had delivered the address, but we were unable to establish that any of the judge's statements influenced TWRA officers to set their cases before the two judges. We did secure one witness, who worked in the boating industry, who claimed to have heard such statements at the dinner but, perhaps because of his employment, the witness backed out of testifying before the trial.

So, in some ways, we lost the battle for McCullough, but eventually we won the war and hopefully assured that other defendants receive a fair trial in a fair tribunal, including all divisions of the Hamilton County General Sessions Court.

What I Know

1. "Judge shopping" is the practice of manipulating the selection of a judge for the purpose of obtaining a decisionmaker likely to be favorable to one party in a case.

2. Judge shopping violates fundamental fairness and due process of law because it may place one party at an advantage, while denying the other party the right to a fair trial before a neutral and detached judge. If a judge is biased in favor of or against one party of the case, the proceeding is fundamentally flawed and the integrity of the proceeding is undermined.

3. McCullough's lawyer had to perform an incredibly detailed and thorough investigation into how cases were assigned and which courts received the assignment of TWRA cases before undertaking a statistical analysis to establish the disproportionate number of cases being heard by the two judges. Counsel also had to become familiar with the judges' backgrounds and relationship with TWRA officers.

4. A lawyer must have immense courage to raise issues concerning questionable judicial practices, particularly when the lawyer continues to practice in those courts. The lawyer risks undermining his relationship with the judges and, in turn, negatively affecting clients whose cases are assigned to the judges.

5. It is appropriate that judicial conduct rules prohibit not only impropriety but also the appearance of impropriety. The public's confidence in the judicial system is essential to assuring the system's legitimacy as a dispute resolution system. When an objective viewer perceives an injustice or observes an appearance of impropriety, the integrity of the system is weakened and public confidence is eroded.

6. Lawyers can sometimes win and lose simultaneously. Here, for example, the lawyer's client was convicted, but by raising the issue of

the allocation of TWRA cases, the lawyer exposed an unfair practice, thereby ensuring that others would not be subject to the practice. Additionally, it is likely that the client received a more favorable plea offer – with the prosecution dismissing multiple charge – than he otherwise would have received.

Chapter XXIII
United States v. Long, 457 Fed. Appx. 534 (6th Cir. 2012)
531 Fed. Appx. 669 (6th Cir.),
cert. denied, 571 U.S. 982 (2013)

1. What were the issues that counsel raised on the two separate appeals in this case?

2. What is a motion for reduction of sentence?

3. How was the judge impacted by mandatory minimum sentencing guidelines?

4. What is a below-guidelines sentence?

CHAPTER XXIII

UNITED STATES v. LONG
457 Fed. Appx. 534 (6th Cir. 2012)
531 Fed. Appx 669 (6th Cir.), cert. denied, 571 U.S. 982 (2013)

At the top of my list of the most tragic cases of my legal career is the criminal prosecution and sentencing of William H. "Billy" Long, former Sheriff of Hamilton County. Billy had served in law enforcement for over thirty years, first as a deputy sheriff and then rising through the ranks to the position of lieutenant in the Hamilton County Sheriff's Department. In a political upset, Billy defeated incumbent Republican Sheriff John Cupp in August 2006, and became sheriff and the rising star of the Hamilton County Democratic Party.

On March 20, 2007, an agent with the Federal Bureau of Investigation (FBI) was interviewing Eugene Overstreet, a funeral home operator and preacher, during an investigation into possible public corruption unrelated to Sheriff Long. During the interview, Overstreet, who had a prior felony conviction, received a call from Sheriff Long. The agent overheard the two discussing an unpaid campaign contribution. When questioned, Overstreet told the agent that he was helping Sheriff Long collect the unpaid debt from convenience store operators, whose stores sold methamphetamine precursors and paid off on video poker machines. According to Overstreet, the campaign contributions were to be made in exchange for protecting the store owners from prosecution.

The FBI began investigating Sheriff Long, introducing undercover agents to pose as store owners and prompting a cooperating witness to seek Long's assistance in laundering proceeds from drug trafficking. Long and Overstreet split various sums of cash furnished by the government. These transactions were recorded by either Overstreet or government agents. During one interaction between the two men, Overstreet, wearing an arm cast provided by the FBI, asked Long to load ten kilograms of cocaine into the trunk of Overstreet's car so that

Overstreet could travel to the drop location and pick up a payment. The drugs were wrapped in a Mexican newspaper and stored in a beer box and, thus, were not visible to Long. Apparently, this ruse was to assure that Long actually touched the drugs.

In February 2008, Long was charged in a twenty-eight count indictment, which included charges of extortion, money laundering, providing a firearm and ammunition to a convicted felon, possession with intent to distribute over five kilograms of cocaine, and possession of a firearm during a drug-trafficking offense. *United States v. Long*, 457 Fed. Appx. 534, 535-36 (6th Cir. 2012). Because of the overwhelming proof and the strict federal sentencing laws, Billy Long plead guilty to twenty-seven counts and was sentenced by United States District Court Judge Harry Sandlin "Sandy" Mattice, Jr.[1] to fourteen years (168 months) in a federal penitentiary that could provide protection for a convicted law enforcement officer. Although we argued vigorously that no prior Tennessee sheriff had been given a sentence in excess of five years, Judge Mattice found that Long has damaged the public trust in local government and deserved a longer sentence. *Id.* at 539.

We challenged the length of the sentence on appeal to the United States Court of Appeals for the Sixth Circuit and were successful. The appellate court held that the trial court had erroneously calculated the base offense levels for the drug trafficking and money-laundering offenses because the conduct "did not involve an offense that could lead to a criminal conviction." *Id.* at 542 (relying on *United States v. Shafer*, 199 F.3d 826, 830 (6th Cir. 1999)). When we returned to Judge Mattice's court in 2012 for resentencing, we were able to establish that Billy had been a model prisoner, was repentant, and had accepted responsibility for his actions. Judge Mattice reduced the sentence to approximately eleven years (135 months).

---

1 At the time of sentencing, Judge Mattice was a relatively new appointee to the federal bench, having been confirmed in 2005. Judge Mattice had been a partner in a prominent Chattanooga law firm for twenty years before being named to serve as Senior Counsel for the United States Senate Committee on Governmental Affairs, working with the late Republican Senator Fred Thompson. In 2001, President George W. Bush appointed Mattice to serve as the United States Attorney for the Eastern District of Tennessee.

When the government refused to support our request for a further sentence reduction based on the "substantial assistance" Billy had provided to the government, we filed a second appeal. This time we argued that the government's refusal was vindictive and based on our disclosure of Overstreet as the government's informant and our aggressive attack on Overstreet's credibility. In a second opinion, *United States v. Long*, 531 Fed. Appx 669 (6th Cir.), *cert. denied*, 571 U.S. 982 (2013), the federal appeals court affirmed the sentence.

A year later, Marya Schalk and I filed a motion for reduction of sentence, based on an amendment to the United States Sentencing Guidelines reducing the offense range for cocaine offenses. Judge Mattice eventually reduced Billy's sentence to ten years (120 months), the lowest sentence he could impose under the mandatory minimum guidelines without the government's request for a below-guideline sentence.

In this case, the substantial work that Marya and I did on Long's case, which included two federal appeals and the filing of a petition for certiorari in the United States Supreme Court, was not performed because of a lucrative and substantial fee but rather because of our strong conviction that our client was receiving disparate treatment. Our client lost the retirement he had accumulated from his thirty-one years of service in law enforcement. Employment opportunities would not be readily available to Long as a convicted felon and ex-law enforcement officer when he was ultimately released from prison. But Marya and I both felt that Billy's initial sentence was disparate to that imposed upon other sheriffs in Tennessee in similar circumstances. We both thought that Billy Long was unfairly treated by the justice system. Combining Marya's brilliance and my stubbornness, we were finally able to achieve some measure of justice for our client that would make up for the lack of financial reward. Billy would eventually be required to serve eighty-five percent (85%) of his sentence, after receiving credit for time served while in a halfway house after his arrest.

What I Know

1. In this case, the appeals concerned the length of the sentence that was imposed. The federal sentencing guidelines are a complex group of statutes that federal judges follow in determining sentences. Counsel was successful in the first appeal because the trial judge had miscalculated the sentence. Although the judge reduced the sentence slightly when the case was returned for resentencing, counsel argued that the judge should grant a further reduction because Long had accepted responsibility and had substantially assisted the government. When the government refused to support the request, counsel appealed again, this time asserting that the government was acting vindictively. This appeal was unsuccessful.

2. A motion for reduction of sentence requests that the judge reduce a previously imposed sentence based on some new circumstances. In this case, the motion for reduction of sentence was filed after Congress changed the sentencing guidelines in a manner that affected Long's sentence.

3. At the time Long was sentenced, the judge was bound to certain mandatory minimum sentencing guidelines. This meant that the judge could not sentence below those guidelines unless the government requested that the judge do so.

4. A below-guidelines sentence is a sentence that falls below the guidelines set out for the offense in the federal sentencing guidelines. At the time of Long's case, a below-guidelines sentence could only be imposed with the government's consent.

Chapter XXIV
In re Estate of Brock, 536 S.W.3d 409 (Tenn. 2017)

1. What do the circumstances of this case indicate about factors that lead people to choose particular lawyers when they need representation?

2. What does it mean to be "disinherited?"

3. What does "testamentary capacity" mean?

4. What is meant by the concept of "standing?"

5. What is a will contest?

6. What do the circumstances of this case say about the relationships between trial courts and appellate courts?

7. What compelled the trial court and appellate court to follow precedent given their expressed reservations with the results?

8. How do lawyers challenge precedent when the case is before a court that is required to follow precedent?

9. What does this case demonstrate about how lawyers undertake to change the law?

CHAPTER XXIV

IN RE ESTATE OF BROCK
536 S.W. 3d 409 (Tenn. 2017)

Don Brock, a 1957 graduate of Chattanooga Central High School, founded Astec Industries in 1972 and developed it into a billion-dollar, multi-national company with eighteen subsidiaries throughout the world. Brock acquired a Ph.D. in mechanical engineering from Georgia Tech and held more than one hundred registered patents associated with asphalt manufacturing plants, paving equipment, and other related products. He served as CEO of Astec until he developed mesothelioma in May 2012 and died on March 10, 2015.

For more than thirty years, Brock was married to Lynne W. Brock. During the couple's marriage, they adopted seven children, included five siblings. The parties' separation led to a bitterly contested divorce in 1993 with charges of adultery on both sides and challenges to the division of approximately one hundred million dollars ($100,000,000). The divorce was final in 1997 after an appeal to the Tennessee Court of Appeals. *Brock v. Brock*, 941 S.W.2d 896 (Tenn. Ct. App. 1996).

During his lifetime, Don executed several wills, gradually minimizing the inheritance of the five adopted siblings, finally eliminating one, Walter, entirely from the will. The other four were to receive lesser amounts than the first two children Don had adopted and less than the children of his second wife, born of her first marriage.

Brock's October 1, 2013 will named his second wife, Sammye Brock, and W. Norman Smith, his lifetime friend and director and co-founder of Astec, as his co-executors. The 2013 will explicitly disinherited each of the five siblings. The 2013 will was filed for probate on March 31, 2015, following Brock's death on March 10.

When one of the five disinherited siblings sought my help in the case, I explained that I had limited experience in the area of will contests, trusts, and estate planning. I was curious why he had contacted me. His reply was one that appeals to an old lawyer's ego. He stated, "Because you are the only one who will help us and is strong enough to take on Astec and the family." Having my ego pumped up I told him I would look into his case and get back with him. After talking to the other lawyers in the firm, who also did not have experience with will contests, I made the wise decision to associate Attorney David Cunningham from Lafayette, Georgia, who had recently handled, along with Bobby Lee Cook, a will contest involving a large estate in the Hamilton County Chancery Court.

We contested the 2013 will on the grounds that it had been improperly executed and that, at the time of execution, Brock lacked the necessary capacity to execute a will (known as "testamentary capacity"). We specifically challenged the authenticity of Don Brock's signature, which appeared only on the last page of the 2013 will, and his testamentary capacity, at the time of execution, based on his fatal illness. We also alleged that Brock's second wife, Sammye, and the two first-adopted children, had conspired to defraud Brock and exerted influence to convince him to disinherit the other five children, who had been unaware of their disinheritance under the 2013 will until after their father's death.

Thus, the long-drawn-out legal battle began!

The Estate of Don Brock was ably represented by Attorney Richard Bethea and others of the Chambliss law firm in Chattanooga. Richard Bethea had represented Don Brock both personally and professionally for many years and had successfully represented Astec and its international subsidiaries in complex litigation.

The Probate Division of the Hamilton County Chancery Court initially held that our clients had "standing" to contest the 2013 will and transferred the case to the Hamilton County Circuit Court, Division 3, for trial. Thereafter, the Estate presented a newly discovered will, appropriately executed in 2012, which also disinherited the five siblings. Based on the 2012 will and armed with two Tennessee Supreme Court cases,[1] the Estate requested that the court reconsider whether the five siblings had standing to challenge Brock's wills.

We took the next step of amending our allegations to contest the validity of the 2012 will, as well as additional wills dated 2006, 1998, and 1994. Although all five siblings had also been disinherited under the 2012 will, only two of the siblings were excluded under the 2006 and 1998 wills and only one was excluded under the 1994 will. In the event all five wills were determined to be invalid, the five disinherited siblings would be entitled to inheritance through the legal mechanism known as "intestate succession," the means by which property is distributed when a person dies without a will.

The Estate relied on cases in which wills were challenged after a court had already determined the validity of the will. Since no court had determined the validity of any of Brock's wills, we argued that those cases did not apply. The judge, though confessing to be "extremely troubled that the status of the Tennessee law in its current form is harsh[,] neither fair nor equitable, and promotes the potential for fraud by simply creating two wills and [having] one insulate the other," found that our clients did not have standing to challenge the wills. *In re Estate of Brock,* 536 S.W.3d 409, 413 (Tenn. 2017) (quoting the lower court judge). The judge based the decision on the 2012 will, which appeared valid on its face, and also disinherited the five siblings. *Id.* Therefore, the five siblings would receive nothing from their father's estate.

On behalf of the disinherited children, we appealed to the Tennessee Court of Appeals, which in a ten-page opinion carefully reviewed the many cases that had arisen since the 1906 precedent relied upon by the lower court. *In re Estate of Brock,* 2016 WL 6503696 (Tenn. Ct. App. Nov. 3, 2016), *perm. to appeal granted,* (Tenn. 2017). Though also "troubled" by the result, the intermediate appellate court

---

1 The two cases constituting legal precedent in the case were *Cowan v. Walker,* 96 S.W. 96 (Tenn. 1906) and *Jennings v. Bridgeford* 403 S.W. 2d 289 (Tenn. 1966).

was "bound to follow [Tennessee Supreme Court decisions] if they are on point" and, thus, agreed with the lower court and affirmed the dismissal of the siblings' will contest case. *Id.* at *6. Nonetheless, the Court of Appeals, like the judge below, encouraged the Tennessee Supreme Court to reexamine the "practical application" of the case precedents and raised disturbing questions: "[l]ike the trial court, we are troubled that standing could potentially be used by a wrongdoer to insulate his or her wrongdoing from being challenged. What stops a wrongdoer, who procures a will by either undue influence or other fraudulent means, from procuring a second will in order to insulate the last from review by the courts?" *Id.*

The Tennessee Supreme Court accepted our application for permission to appeal and reversed the two lower courts' decisions. The late Justice Cornelia Clark issued the opinion of the Court:

> We reaffirm the general rule, long recognized in Tennessee, that to establish standing a contestant must show that he or she would be entitled to share in the decedent's estate if the will were set aside or if no will existed. The contestants here have satisfied this requirement by showing that they would share in the decedent's estate under the laws of intestacy and under prior wills.

When the case was sent back to Hamilton County Chancery Court to commence lengthy, expensive, and nasty litigation, the parties reached a non-disclosed confidential settlement. While the settlement likely did not satisfy either side, it saved everyone years of fiercely contested and expensive litigation. As the old cliché goes "a settlement which pleases no one is probably a good settlement."

What I Know

1. The circumstances of this case indicate that a lawyer's reputation in the community is an important factor that people consider when searching for lawyers. As was true in this case, clients often seek lawyers who have the reputation for zealously representing their clients. These clients wanted a lawyer who would fight for them and not cower when faced with strong and powerful opposition.

2. When an individual is "disinherited," the individual is excluded from receiving proceeds from another person's will. For example, if a parent drafts a valid will that excludes one or more children, those children have been disinherited and will not receive anything from the parent's estate when the parent dies.

3. "Testamentary capacity" refers to the legal ability and mental capability to execute a valid will.

4. "Standing" refers to the capacity of an individual or entity to file a lawsuit in court, usually based on some identifiable interest in the matter. Generally, an individual who has suffered harm by another's actions has standing to file suit.

5. A will contest is a formal objection challenging the validity of a will. Will contests may be based on the assertion that the testator, the party who made the will, did not have the testamentary capacity to execute a will. Will contests can also be based on allegations that a testator was unduly influenced or subjected to fraud or coercion.

6. Trial courts are bound to follow appellate court decisions even when they disagree with the outcome. As indicated in this case, trial judges may express concern in their decisions about the unfairness of precedent, which may in turn convince the appellate court to reconsider the appropriateness of the precedent.

7. The principle of stare decisis compelled the trial and appellate courts to make their decisions despite their reservations.

8. Lawyers challenge precedent in lower courts by objecting and raising the issue for appellate review.

9. Lawyers who want to change the law through litigation must be prepared to lose in the lower courts, while carefully preserving every issue for appeal. On appeal, lawyers should also demonstrate how the existing law is unfair or inequitable, or how it might encourage improper behavior.

Chapter XXV
State v. Franklin, 2018 WL 3998766
(Tenn. Crim. App. Aug. 21, 2018)

1. How do the courts balance the tension between the goals of public safety and the rights of individuals?

2. What is the purpose of giving notice to the media about upcoming roadblocks?

3. How does advance public notice of a roadblock provide deterrence?

4. Why did the presence of "unfettered" individual officer discretion undermine the propriety of the roadblock in this case?

5. Why is it important to post signs to alert motorists that they are approaching a roadblock?

CHAPTER XXV

STATE v. FRANKLIN
2018 WL 3998766 (Tenn. Crim. App. Aug. 21, 2018)

On June 15, 2012, from 11:00 p.m. until 12:30 a.m., Tennessee Highway Patrol (THP) District Captain (Cpt.) David McGill requested authority to conduct a sobriety checkpoint on Cherokee Boulevard just west of the two-lane Stringers Ridge Tunnel in the North Chattanooga area. The checkpoint was conducted to coincide with the time that the annual Riverbend Music Festival would be concluding, and the large crowd in attendance would be driving home.

Robert Franklin had left the festival early to beat the crowd but was stopped at the checkpoint just as he came through the tunnel. When asked, Franklin said that he had been drinking. He was then directed to pull over and perform some field sobriety tests that the officers alleged that Franklin failed. After delay, Franklin was charged with driving under the influence (DUI) and registered a blood alcohol concentration in excess of the statutory presumption.

As we had done in previous cases, *see* Chapters XVII & XIX, *supra*, we challenged the sobriety checkpoint arguing that it violated the Fourth Amendment of the United States Constitution and Article l, Section 7 of the Tennessee Constitution. At a hearing, Cpt. David McGill testified that he had completed a THP Checkpoint Request/Authorization Form ("form") and received approval from Lieutenant Wayne Springer, his supervising officer, to conduct the sobriety checkpoint. The form was signed, dated, and approved approximately two and one-half years before the checkpoint was conducted based on concerns at the time about crashes on a parallel highway that was not conducive to a checkpoint.

The form stated that "all personnel participating … will be responsible for following procedures outlined in General Order 410-1." The form also ordered that motorists would be "momentarily stopped" at the checkpoint. Additionally, the form indicated that the media had been informed to give advance notice of the checkpoint.

In addition to establishing that no advance media notice had been given, we presented testimony of two witnesses who were not stopped at the checkpoint; moreover, one witness testified that she did not see any indication or warning of a checkpoint before entering the tunnel and seeing flashing blue lights. The thrust of the defense was that the lack of advance media publicity and adequate warning signs violated General Order 410-1 and resulted in an unreasonable seizure of motorists without probable cause.

The trial court denied our challenge to the checkpoint, emphasizing that the government had a compelling interest in enforcing laws aims at deterring drivers from driving after consuming alcoholic beverages. We asked the court to reconsider its ruling and offered our client's testimony, challenging a Red Bank police officer's testimony that motorists had avoided the roadblock by turning onto a nearby street. The trial court denied reconsideration. We later asked the trial judge to dismiss the case or to exclude evidence based on a pending case before the state supreme court, *see* Chapter XXVI *infra*, but we were unsuccessful on that motion as well.

When Franklin's case ultimately went to trial, Franklin testified that he had consumed three drinks and did not think he was impaired. Nonetheless, the jury found him guilty, and he was sentenced to the statutory minimum sentence for a first offense of DUI.

On appeal, the Tennessee Court of Criminal Appeals, with Judge Camille McMullen writing the lengthy compelling opinion, agreed that the sobriety checkpoint violated the standards set down in *State v. Downy*, 945 S.W.2d 102 (Tenn. 1997); moreover, Judge McMullen concluded that "the lack of advance notice, the officers' exercise of substantial discretion at the scene, and the substantial deviations from Order [410-1][1] severely interfered with Franklin's privacy and liberty." *State v. Franklin*, 2018 WL 3998766, *17.

---

1 Judge McMullen listed seven deviations from the operational guidelines of General Order 410-1, including: (1) the site was not selected based on safety and did not ensure adequate visibility; (2) the site did not give adequate advance warning; (3) the deterrent effect was not considered because no advance public notice was given; (4) the lieutenant failed to inspect location to ensure compliance; (5) the captain failed to inspect site to determine if met criteria; (6) the captain did not present press release to the media; and (7) the site supervisor did not enter activity as required and did not submit the required reports.

Judge McMullen identified three factors that would have helped to minimize the risk of arbitrary intrusions on liberty and privacy that were not present at the checkpoint. First, "the officers had exercised nearly unfettered discretion in determining which cars to stop." *Id.* at *20. Second, the officers "failed to warn motorists of the checkpoint before entering the tunnel and failed to stop cars only in a safe and visible area." *Id.* Judge McMullen questioned whether tunnels, "which provide the motorists limited space in which to avoid accidents and place officers and motorists at increased risk of harm, should ever be utilized to conceal checkpoints." *Id.* The circumstances here led the court to conclude that "adequate safety precautions were not taken [thus weighing] against a finding that the checkpoint is constitutionally permissible." Third, "no advance publicity was given to the public at large regarding this checkpoint." *Id.* at 21. While the absence of public notice was not determinative, Judge McMullen noted that the publicity requirement "is a key aspect of a minimally intrusive roadblock." *Id.*

In reversing the trial court's order, Judge McMullen, along with her colleagues Judge Curwood Witt, Jr., and Judge Robert Holloway, Jr., applied and reaffirmed the guidelines of *Downy* and suppressed the evidence resulting from Franklin's stop.[2] The state did not seek permission to appeal and the charges against Franklin were subsequently dismissed.

---

2 The Court of Criminal Appeals referenced its decision in *State v. Decosimo,* 2018 WL 733218 (Tenn. Crim. App. Feb. 6, 2018), *perm to appeal granted,* (Tenn. 2018), *see* Chapter XXVI *infra,* which, along with *State v. Franklin,* raised the issue of the constitutionality of the fee aspects of Tenn. Code Ann. §55-10-413(9). That argument, the statute, and *State v. Decosimo* are discussed thoroughly in Chapter XXVI *infra.*

What I Know

1. Courts balance public safety interests against the rights of individuals by using various levels of discernment to scrutinize the interests. The more the policy infringes on individual rights, the greater public safety interest the policy must serve to justify its existence.

2. The purpose of notifying the media about the time and locations of roadblocks is to give the public notice that if they travel a particular route at a particular time, they will undergo an inconvenience by having their freedom of movement interrupted when they are stopped at the roadblock. If an individual has notice yet chooses to travel the route and be stopped at the roadblock, the government's argument that the roadblock seizure is reasonable is enhanced, and the individual's argument that his rights have been violated is diminished.

3. Advance public notice gives an individual an opportunity to avoid a roadblock or checkpoint. An individual who knows that the police are conducting a roadblock may be deterred from engaging in illegal behavior that the roadblock is established to detect. Additionally, an individual who knows that a roadblock is in a particular location can choose a different route, thereby eliminating exposure to state intrusion without reasonable suspicion of wrongdoing.

4. The exercise of "unfettered" discretion in this case undermined the propriety of the roadblock because it allowed the individual officers to choose which vehicles to stop rather than subjecting them to an established protocol or policy. Allowing officer's unfettered discretion may result in officers exercising their discretion in an impermissible, unfair, or discriminatory manner.

5. It is important to post signs alerting motorists about roadblocks because it gives motorists notice of the upcoming roadblock and allows them to avoid the temporary seizure if they choose to do so.

Chapter XXVI
State v. Decosimo, 555 S.W.3d 494 (Tenn. 2018)

1. What is the basis for counsel's argument that the fees collected under the state law created a "financial incentive to secure convictions?"

2. Why would a law that created a financial incentive undermine the fundamental right to a fair trial?

3. What is a jury instruction? What was the special jury instruction requested and, ultimately, allowed in this case?

4. What is a nolo contendere plea?

5. What is meant by "reserving a certified question of law for appellate review?"

6. Consider whether it is appropriate for judges to consider practical consequences when deciding a matter, such as potential governmental expense and encouragement of other litigation, in reaching a decision and, alternatively, whether it is realistic to expect judges to disregard such consequences.

7. What are some potential legislative reactions to judicial decisions?

8. What factors influence the legislative process?

CHAPTER XXVI

STATE v. DECOSIMO
555 S.W. 3d 494 (Tenn. 2018)

In this driving under the influence (DUI) case, we challenged the constitutionality of a state law that imposed a fee upon convicted DUI offenders when forensic scientists employed by the Tennessee Bureau of Investigation (TBI) tested their blood to determine drug or alcohol content. The statute directed the collected fees to be returned to the TBI for its use.[1] We challenged the statute arguing that the statute gave TBI scientists "a personal and institutional financial incentive to produce blood alcohol test results that secure convictions, which, in turn increases fees and funding for the TBI." *State v. Decosimo*, 555 S.W.3d 494, 496 (Tenn. 2018).

Rosemary Decosimo was arrested in the early hours of August 18, 2012, and charged with DUI and several traffic offenses. Decosimo consented to a blood test, which was analyzed by a forensic scientist for the TBI. The analysis produced a blood alcohol content (BAC) that was twice the legal presumption of intoxication under Tennessee statutes. On behalf of Decosimo, we filed a motion to dismiss or, in the alternative, to suppress evidence of the TBI blood alcohol test results. Our motion alleged that the fee system gave rise to an appearance of impropriety that violated our client's fundamental right to a fair trial guaranteed by both the Due Process Clause of the Fourteenth Amendment to the United States Constitution and Article I, Section 8 of the Tennessee Constitution.

---

1 Tenn. Code Ann. §55-10-413(f)(B) provided for a two hundred and fifty dollar ($250) fee is to be collected for blood alcohol or drug concentration (BADT) tests on individuals convicted of certain offenses, including DUI. The BADT fees are deposited into a TBI testing fund and "shall not revert to the general fund of the [S]tate, but shall remain available for appropriate to the [TBI], as determined by the [G]eneral [A]ssembly." Tenn. Code Ann. §55-10-413(f)(B) (2017).

In addition to our motion on behalf of Decosimo, we filed identical motions on behalf of twenty-six other defendants charged with DUI in each of the three divisions of the Hamilton County Criminal Court. We then requested an en banc hearing before Judge Barry Steelman, Judge Rebecca Stern, and Judge Don Poole, the three judges of the three divisions. The judges granted our motion for an en banc hearing.

Our position was not that the TBI forensic scientists were actually biased, nor did we assert that they were engaged in inappropriate behavior. We explicitly premised our constitutional argument on the "appearance of impropriety" and the "potential" for abuse arising from the financial interest that TBI forensic scientists had in obtaining convictions in order to collect fees from the blood alcohol and drug tests (BADT).

As part of our proof, we introduced the testimony of former TBI Director Mark Gwyn, given before the Tennessee General Assembly's Senate Judiciary Committee in February 2014, as part of his budgetary requests for the TBI. Gwyn summarized the revenue and expenses related to BADT for 2009-2012. During those four years, the fines generated a total surplus in excess of $1,600,000 that Director Gwyn claimed was spent on equipment and training. Claiming deep budget cuts in 2008 he had asked the General Assembly to raise the fees collected from BADT from one hundred dollars ($100) to two hundred fifty dollars ($250). He denied that the TBI special fund created an appearance of impropriety, but he did acknowledge that errors had occurred.[2]

We also presented the testimony of two experienced criminal defense lawyers, Raymond W. Fraley of Fayetteville and Lloyd Levitt of Chattanooga, who testified that they had handled between one thousand and two thousand DUI cases in their careers. Both expressed their opinions that the blood alcohol concentration was the most damaging evidence against a defendant in a DUI case.

---

2 For example, Gwynn admitted that a scientist had switched a sample in a vehicular homicide case in Chattanooga that resulted in almost three thousand cases having to be re-tested with varying results. We were able to show that the variances in the re-tests were such that some of the readings were actually below the presumed intoxication level.

At the conclusion of the hearing, we again emphasized that we had not alleged and were not relying upon claims of intentional bias or manipulation on the part of the TBI scientists. Rather, it was our position that the fundamental right to a fair trial was violated because the system created the appearance of impropriety. After the en banc hearing, the three Hamilton County Criminal Court Judges entered an order denying our motion to dismiss or suppress but granted us the right to have the jury instructed about the potential impact on the credibility of TBI forensic scientists. The order described the TBI's financial interests as "'not negligible' and 'very large' in the aggregate." *Id.* at 503 (quoting the trial judges' order). We sought interlocutory appellate review but were denied review by both the Tennessee Court of Criminal Appeals and the Tennessee Supreme Court.

The statutory fee structure was widely discussed throughout the State and caused a variety of reactions amongst judges, prosecutors, and defense counsel. Some lawyers were able to use the situation to get cases dismissed; others negotiated reduced plea agreements; still others had their cases held in abeyance pending an appellate decision on the issue. Some, of course, ignored the circumstances and carried on with business as usual.

We managed to resolve all the cases included in the en banc hearing except for Decosimo's case. When Senior Judge Paul G. Summers was designated to hear the case, we renewed out motion, relying on the transcript from the en banc hearing and additional testimony and evidence from a March 2015 budget hearings before the General Assembly's Senate Judiciary Committee. That evidence included Department of Revenue data showing that from 2005-2016, revenue from BADT exceeded twenty-two million dollars ($22,000,000) and averaged about three million dollars ($3,000,000) a year. When Judge Summers denied our motion, Decosimo then entered a nolo contendere plea to DUI per se, received the standard minimum sentence for first offense DUI, and reserved the following certified question of law for appellate review:

> Whether the trial court erred in not dismissing the case, or alternatively, suppressing the blood alcohol evidence without which the State could not proceed against the

defendant on this DUI per se conviction, where T.C.A. 55-10-413(f) is unconstitutional in violation of due process and rights to a fair trial under the Fifth, Sixth, and Fourteenth Amendments of the United States Constitution and under article I, sections 8 and 9 of the Tennessee Constitution based on the fact that the [TBI] received a $250 BADT/BAT fee in every case in which a conviction is obtained for driving under the influence or other listed offense, wherein a TBI blood test or TBI-calibrated breath test result is used, thereby creating a "contingent-fee-dependent system" susceptible to bias because the TBI's testing and interpretation of these tests play the determinative role in the prosecution of the charge, and a jury instruction regarding this statutory incentive in favor of conviction is insufficient to cure the magnitude of the constitutional violation.

In a thorough and well-reasoned opinion written by Judge Camille R. McMullen and concurred in by Judge James Curwood Witt, Jr. and Judge Robert L. Holloway, the intermediate appellate court reversed the trial court and declared that Tennessee Code Annotated Section 55-10-413(f) was unconstitutional. *State v. Decosimo*, 2018 WL 733218 (Tenn. Crim. App. Feb. 6, 2018), *rev'd*, 555 S.W.3d 494 (Tenn. 2018). Not unexpectedly, this ruling created a great deal of turmoil and consternation in the legal system. We, of course, anticipated that the State of Tennessee would appeal the decision to the Tennessee Supreme Court, and they did.

In addition to seeking an appeal, the state requested that the Tennessee Supreme Court grant an expedited hearing due to the importance of the decision to the public and the legal system. Between the date of the state's filings and the oral argument, the Tennessee General Assembly amended the statute directing that all BADT fees be paid into the state's general fund.

Whether this change in the law impacted the Tennessee Supreme Court's decision is merely a matter of conjecture. But, without a doubt, the collateral consequences of holding the statute unconstitutional were significant. For example, by reversing the intermediate appellate court's holding, the Tennessee Supreme Court reduced the potential for a class action lawsuit seeking reimbursement for all defendants who had been convicted and paid the BADT fee.[3] The reversal also curtailed the influx of post-conviction petitions filed by convicted defendants raising due process violations based on the fee structure. But by upholding the constitutionality of the statute, the state's general fund would continue to be positively impacted by an increase in DUI convictions.

On August 23, 2018, writing on behalf of a unanimous court, the late Judge Cornelia Clark reversed the Court of Criminal Appeals' decision and affirmed Judge Summers' bench trial judgment. *State v. Decosimo*, 555 S.W.3d 494 (Tenn. 2018). While we earned the concession of the Chief Justice during oral argument that the statute was "bad law," neither the Chief Justice nor the other members of the court believed that the statute violated due process.

The court's opinion included a reference suggesting that we believed the amendment to the statute would remedy its constitutional infirmity. In a footnote in the opinion, Justice Clark stated that

> the defendant has stated throughout this litigation, including in her supplemental brief and again at oral argument before this Court, that amending the statute to deposit BADT fees in the State's general fund rather than earmarking BADT fees to the TBI would eliminate the basis of her constitutional challenge. The 2018 legislation revised the BADT statute in precisely this manner.

Id. at 506 n. 10. Our position was and is just the opposite – the amendment transferring the TBI BADT funds to the state's general fund does not eliminate the constitutional challenge because the statute continues to provide that the BADT fee is collected only when an accused is convicted; thus the incentive to convict that the statute creates is not eliminated simply by transferring the fees to a different state fund.

---

3 An informed source within the Tennessee government stated that the main concern of the government was the potential class action lawsuit that might be prompted should the supreme court uphold the finding that Tennessee Code Annotated Section 55-10-413(f) was unconstitutional. A second informed source also stated that this was a concern to at least one member of the Tennessee Supreme Court.

We attempted without success to appeal the case to the United States Supreme Court, so the legal battle that began on August 18, 2012, with the arrest of Rosemary Decosimo ended with Justice Clark's opinion entered on August 23, 2018. Or did it? Does the amended provision imposing a two hundred fifty dollar ($250) fee after conviction, in those cases in which the TBI forensic scientist performs the BADT violate due process and fundamental fairness? Do those convicted individuals who contributed to the millions of dollars collected by TBI under the former statute have a legally cognizable claim? With tenacious lawyers, time will tell.

What I Know

1. The basis of the argument that the fee incentivized TBI to produce convictions is simply this: because the TBI collected the fee only when an accused was convicted, there was a financial incentive to assure that the BADT indicated sufficient alcohol or drug content to sustain a conviction. This financial incentive created, at a minimum, an appearance of impropriety in that the TBI stood to gain, literally, only when the test results led to convictions.

2. A law that creates a financial incentive undermines the right to a fair trial because it suggests that the outcome of a case may be influenced by factors other than the facts and the law.

3. A jury instruction is the statement of the law that the judge gives to the jury and which the jury must follow in deciding the case. In this case, the three-judge panel granted the defense request for a special jury instruction. The instruction allowed the jury to consider whether the statutory fee structure with its potential to benefit the TBI impacted the credibility of the TBI scientists who were conducting the BADT and the reliability of the test results they provided.

4. A nolo contendre or "no contest" plea is an accused's plea that does not admit guilt, but also does not challenge the prosecution's case. When an accused pleads nolo contendere, the accused is sentenced as though a guilty plea had been entered.

5. To "reserve a certified question of law for appellate review" means that the accused offers either a conditional guilty or nolo contendere plea, subject to the determination of a legal issue on appeal. If the legal issue is determined in the accused's favor, and is dispositive of the case, the accused may withdraw the guilty plea and move forward with trial or further plea negotiations. If the legal issue is resolved

against the accused, the guilty or nolo contendere plea and the sentence stands.

6. Whether it is proper for judges to consider practical consequences in making their decisions depends on who you ask. Some say that it is inevitable because judges are human, and thus not exempt from living in a world with finite time and finite resources. Others say that it would be improper for judges to weigh any consideration other than the facts presented by the parties and the applicable law. What is most essential is that the judge apply the law in a neutral and fair manner and resist being swayed by public pressure and political considerations.

7. The primary way legislatures react to judicial decisions is by changing the law, as happened in this case.

8. Factors that influence the legislative process include the interests, desires, and demands of the electorate, influence exerted by special interest groups, a legislator's political viewpoint and personal preferences, research, and constituent feedback.

Chapter XXVII
Death Penalty Cases

State v. Edmond, No. 129132 (Tenn. Crim. App. Aug. 22), *pet. for cert. denied,* (Tenn. Oct. 1, 1977)[1]

State v. Pritchett, 621 S.W.2d 127 (Tenn.), *reh. denied,* (Tenn. 1981)

Dyer v. State, 1995 WL 141565 (Tenn. Crim. App. April 3), *perm. to app. denied,* (Tenn. 1995).

1. What has been the history of capital punishment in the United States?

2. How does the United States Supreme Court rulings on the constitutionality of capital punishment impact the death penalty in Tennessee and other states?

3. What factors does a jury consider in determining whether to impose a death sentence?

4. How do "aggravating circumstances" and "mitigating circumstances" affect whether a death sentence is imposed?

5. What might motivate a judge to refuse to accept an agreement between the prosecution and the defense to sentence a defendant to a life sentence?

---

1 This case does not have a Westlaw citation, but all pertinent documents are on file in the author's office.

6. What is the Ex Post Facto Clause and how was it implicated in the *Dyer* case?

7. Does the *Dyer* case offer any explanation for why proceedings in capital cases often last for decades?

CHAPTER XXVII

DEATH PENALTY CASES

In only four out of the many first-degree murder cases I have tried over my fifty-six year career has the possibility of a jury rendering a death sentence been a serious concern. One of those cases, *State v. Griffey,* discussed in Chapter IX, *supra,* is a prime example of how two juries can differ so greatly in their verdicts. The other three cases in which the death penalty was at issue are discussed below.

1. EDMOND V. STATE, NO. 129132 (Tenn. Crim. App. Aug. 22), *pet. cert. denied,* (Tenn. Oct. 1, 1977)

Janet Edmond, a young, attractive woman, shot her husband twice with a shotgun while the two were at the lounge they operated on Dobbs Avenue in downtown Chattanooga. The proof was undisputed that the defendant went to the night club on September 24, 1974, armed with a shotgun and shot her husband. Prior to the shooting, the defendant told her mother that she was going to "blow the SOB in two."

Anticipating that we could get a bad verdict but hoping for a reduced sentence for manslaughter or a finding of self-defense, we challenged the constitutionality of the Tennessee death penalty statute and attacked the grand jury selection process, which at the time unconstitutionally excluded women, attorneys, physicians, pharmacists, and others who affirmatively requested an exemption from service.

The trial judge, Campbell Carden, denied both motions and the case went to trial. Edmond admitted that she shot her husband, but claimed self-defense, offering proof that her husband was found with a pistol near his body. During her trial, she showed no emotion or regret and the jury, ultimately, rejected her claim of self-defense, convicted her of first-degree murder, and sentenced her to death. The trial judge, in an extraordinary decision, not only allowed the defendant to remain free on bond pending a hearing on the motion for new trial but set an appeal bond of only five thousand dollars ($5,000) after denying the motion for new trial.

On August 22, 1977, the Tennessee Court of Criminal Appeals overruled all of our appellate issues, except the one challenging the death penalty and set an additional appeal bond in the amount of ten thousand dollars ($10,000). By the time the appellate court issued its opinion, Tennessee Governor Ray Blanton had commuted all death sentences in the state to life imprisonment. The appellate court concluded its opinion noting Governor Blanton's actions and stated that the "judgment as commuted is affirmed." *State v. Edmond*, No. 129132, at page 9 (Tenn. Crim. App. Aug. 22, 1977), *pet. cert. denied*, (Tenn. Oct. 1, 1977). We asked the Tennessee Supreme Court to review the case, but they refused to grant an appeal. *Id.*

Reportedly, Janet Edmond eventually received a reduction in her sentence. In hindsight, we probably should have sought review in the United States Supreme Court on the constitutionality of the grand jury exemptions, as that issue ultimately received attention in the High Court.

I asked Judge Campbell Carden, in the later years of his judicial career, why he set such a low appeal bond in the Edmond case, and he stated that he "just didn't feel right about the verdict."

2. STATE v. PRITCHETT, 621 S.W.2d 127 (Tenn.), *reh. denied*, (Tenn. 1981)

Sandra McCrea and I were hired by the defendant's family to appeal his conviction of first-degree murder in the Circuit Court of Marion County, which occurred while he was represented by court-appointed counsel. Pritchett had been convicted of shooting a taxi driver, in the back of his head with a pump shotgun, while riding in the backseat. The jury sentenced Pritchett to death finding that the murder was aggravated by two "aggravating circumstances." First, the jury found that the murder was "especially heinous, atrocious, or cruel in that it involved torture or depravity of mind." Second, the jury found that the murder was committed "while the defendant was engaged in committing robbery." *State v. Pritchett*, 621 S.W.2d 127, 130 (Tenn. 1981).

In challenging Pritchett's conviction, we argued that his constitutional right to due process was violated because his preliminary hearing was presided over by a non-lawyer judge. We also raised challenges to the constitutionality of Tennessee's death penalty and questioned the aggravating circumstances used to sentence him to death.

The Tennessee Supreme Court ultimately ruled that the facts of Pritchett's case did not satisfy the requirement of the first aggravating circumstance, requiring that the killing be especially heinous, atrocious, or cruel. Because the proof showed that the victim's death was caused instantaneously by the first gunshot wound to the head, the firing of the second shot did not involve torture or depravity of mind; thus, the murder was not "especially heinous, atrocious or cruel." *Id.* at 139.

When the case was remanded for Pritchett to be resentenced, the prosecutor, Bill Pope, agreed with us that the defendant should receive a sentence of life imprisonment with parole, but the trial judge, Judge Paul Swafford, would not accept the recommendation. The prosecutor and the judge disagreed on who had the final authority when the prosecution and defense sought an agreed-to sentence. We were granted an interlocutory appeal on that issue and learned, through the appellate opinion that the final authority whether to accept or reject the proposed disposition of the case rested with the trial judge.

Because Judge Swafford would not accept the recommended disposition of the case, we retried the sentencing before a jury. During that sentencing hearing, the district attorney encouraged the jury to give Pritchett a life sentence. Ultimately, the jury could not reach a unanimous verdict and the court declared a mistrial. We then resolved the case with a life sentence and the standard right to parole. Throughout my career, I tried many murder cases with the *Pritchett* prosecutor, the late William J. Pope, Jr. of Pikeville, Tennessee. He was a fair but tough prosecutor and I always respected in particular the position he took in the *Pritchett* resentencing.

3. DYER v. STATE, 1995 WL 141565 (Tenn. Crim. App. April 3), *perm. to appeal denied*, (Tenn. 1995)

In 1975, Joe Dyer, and a co-defendant Logan, were charged with the murder of two University of Chattanooga students over a drug deal gone bad. Dyer shot both of the victims, one of whom was from a very prominent family, and buried them in a shallow grave at the Chattanooga Rifle Club off Hunter Road in Hamilton County. The bodies were discovered after animals partially uncovered the remains, allowing a hand to protrude from the grave.

The prosecution allowed Dyer's co-defendant to become a state's witness and sentenced Logan to ten years for testifying against Dyer. Dyer was convicted on two counts of first-degree murder and two counts of grand larceny and sentenced to death. When the Tennessee death penalty statute was declared unconstitutional during the pendency of his appeal, Dyer's sentence was commuted to life imprisonment. *Dyer v. State*, 1995 WL 141565 (Tenn. Crim. App. April 3, 1995), *perm. to appeal denied*, (Tenn. 1995); see *Dyer v. Tennessee Board of Paroles*, 2001 WL 401596 (Tenn. Ct. App. April 23, 2001), *perm. app. denied*, (Tenn. 2001).

Although we did not represent Dyer in further legal proceedings, his involvement with the legal system continued. Political pressure by the local district attorney's office along with pressure from one of the victim's families, led to a continuous battle with the parole board. At Dyer's first parole hearing in 1993, his request for parole was denied due to the seriousness of the offense. Thereafter, the parole board consistently denied parole by applying the parole regulations in effect at the time of his second parole hearing, rather than the ones in effect at the time of his offense. Dyer challenged the parole board's actions, arguing that the actions violated both the Ex Post Facto and Due Process Clauses of the United States Constitution. But, ultimately, the Tennessee courts denied his claims.

Dyer, acting as his own lawyer, then filed for relief in federal court, raising the same constitutional issues he had raised in state court. The United States District Court for the Eastern District of Tennessee denied Dyer's request. When Dyer appealed to the United States Court of Appeals for the Sixth Circuit, the panel, in an opinion written by Judge Ronald Gilman, reversed the district court and remanded the case for further proceedings. *Dyer v. Bowlen*, 465 F.3d 280 (6th Cir. 2006). But on remand, District Judge R. Allan Edgar denied relief with the rather cryptic comment, "[t]his case has a long and tortured past. The time has now come to put it to rest." *Dyer v. Morrow*, 2010 WL 199986, *1 (E.D. Tenn. Jan. 13, 2010), *aff'd*, 499 Fed. Appx. 505 (6th Cir. 2012), *cert. denied*, 568 U.S. 1217 (2013).

This time, when Dyer appealed, he received appointed counsel, the Honorable Tom Greenholtz, who later served as a judge of Division Il of the Hamilton County Criminal Court and now serves as a 2022 appointee to the Tennessee Court of Criminal Appeals. The Sixth Circuit disagreed that the case should be put to rest, choosing instead to "resurrect it" so that the Tennessee courts could resolve the issue of whether the correct parole regulations were applied in Dyer's 2009 parole hearing. *Dyer v. Morrow*, 499 Fed. Appx. 505, 506 (6th Cir. 2012), *cert. denied*, 568 U.S. 1217 (2013). Once Dyer invoked and exhausted other remedies to determine that issue, he perhaps again could seek relief in the federal courts. Dyer and his appointed counsel chose to file a petition for writ of certiorari to the United States Supreme Court, which was denied on March 4, 2013. *Dyer v. Morrow*, 568 U.S. 1217 (2013). Dyer was released from the Tennessee Department of Corrections on January 31, 2014, after a parole board hearing on December 19, 2013, and he now resides in Hamilton County.

What I Know

1. Capital punishment has existed from the founding of the United States. Because the Fifth Amendment refers to "capital crimes," it has been presumed that capital punishment, under appropriate circumstances, is constitutional. In 1972, the Supreme Court of the United States found that capital punishment, as administered in the United States, violated constitutional requirements, but since that time the Court has consistently upheld various state capital punishment schemes. Notwithstanding this endorsement of capital punishment, public sentiment for the ultimate penalty appears to be at an all-time low.

2. The United States Supreme Court's rulings in death penalty cases generally are based on the Eighth Amendment's prohibition against cruel and unusual punishments. Because that constitutional prohibition applies to the states, the United States Supreme Court's capital punishment jurisprudence binds every state, including Tennessee.

3. In most jurisdictions, in deciding whether to impose the death penalty, a jury considers aggravating and mitigating circumstances as defined by state law.

4. In many states, including Tennessee, the jury must consider and weigh aggravating and mitigating circumstances, in deciding the sentence for a defendant who has been found guilty of a capital crime. Aggravating circumstances include circumstances that worsen the crime or the offender, while mitigating circumstances are those that lessen culpability. For example, in Tennessee, the following circumstances may be considered as aggravating circumstances: age of victims, number of victims, vulnerability of victims, status of victims, prior convictions of the defendant, violent nature of the murder, murder was committed during the commission of another felony, and

others. Mitigating circumstances may include the defendant's age, mental and physical capacity, social and educational background, and any other factor that should be considered to diminish the culpability of the defendant.

5. A judge might be motivated to refuse to accept a plea agreement to a life sentence because the judge believes that the crime warrants a death sentence or because the judge believes that the jury is better situated to decide the appropriate punishment.

6. The Ex Post Facto Clause of the United States Constitution prohibits ex post facto laws. An ex post facto law retroactively changes the legal consequences of actions or relationships that existed before the law was enacted. In criminal law, the Ex Post Facto Clause prohibits the legislature from criminalizing actions that were legal at the time they were committed and from increasing punishment by adding new penalties or enhancing existing ones and applying the increased punishments to acts that occurred before the change in the law. The Clause also prohibits applying changes in the legal requirements for an offense retroactively. In *Dyer*, the accused argued that the parole board violated the Ex Post Facto Clause by applying parole regulations that were not in effect at the time of Dyer's offense.

7. The *Dyer* case demonstrates why capital cases often involve decades of litigation. As the United States Supreme Court has often stated, capital punishment is unique in its severity and its finality. Once imposed, it is simply irrevocable. Thus, it is critically important that the process have a heightened degree of reliability. The number of appellate review processes that are available may delay execution, but they may also exonerate an accused, thus saving an innocent person from execution. Though the lengthy appellate processes delay execution, they are vital and necessary to assure that every death sentence is imposed fairly and in accord with due process of law.

CONCLUSION

While the cases described in this book have provided a variety of examples of winning and losing at trial and on appeal and emphasized the importance of hoping to win while preparing to lose, the vital message is the importance of the assistance of counsel and the value – and honor – of being a zealous, competent advocate for your client. Our adversary system of justice depends on lawyers serving as able advocates for all parties to litigation, no matter whether the parties are beloved or detested.

Although the right to counsel is only guaranteed in criminal cases, as this book has demonstrated, the presence of counsel's guiding hand is equally important in civil matters. Sometimes, in compelling circumstances, a judge may ask a lawyer to take on a case or a client. Early in my career, I was asked by Hamilton County Chancellor (later Tennessee Court of Appeals Judge) Herschel Franks to take a case involving a notorious inmate who was serving a life sentence in the old Tennessee State Penitentiary, affectionately called the "Tombs." James Earl Ray, who had plead guilty to killing Dr. Martin Luther King, Jr., in Memphis, had become displeased with his lawyers, including notable Texas lawyer, Percy Foreman. Ray filed a pro se petition asking the Hamilton County Chancery Court to require counsel to return Ray's files. Ray was entitled to his files – files are a client's property – but he was having no luck getting them, so he turned to the court, where he had a right to legal recourse despite his criminal record.

Chancellor Franks knew me and my practice and, according to what he told me, he believed that I might be able to represent Ray without the representation destroying my legal career. I negotiated the return of Ray's files and traveled to Nashville in October, 1972, to meet Ray, deliver the files, and secure his written permission to dismiss his chancery suit. After I gave the file to Ray, he looked at it but did not say a word. I was concerned, so I asked him whether something was wrong. After a pause, Ray looked at me and said, "No, Mr. Summers, it is just the first time I ever won anything in a court of law."

On another occasion, an equally infamous client, Byron De La Beckwith, called my office to request my services. In 1990, De La Beckwith was indicted and was facing a third trial in Mississippi for the 1963 death of civil rights leader, Medgar Evans. At the time, De La Beckwith was living in Signal Mountain, Tennessee.

When De La Beckwith called, he encouraged me to take his case for free, assuring me that I could gain a "national reputation," to go along with my local and state reputation by representing him. I am unclear whether I set him straight on my "national reputation," but I am sure that I gave him some free legal advice to the effect that he should immediately return in secret to Mississippi.

I told him, "Turn yourself over to the judicial authorities in that state before the Tennessee governor signs the extradition warrant; otherwise you will be held without bond." De La Beckwith ignored that advice, was arrested, held without bond, tried and convicted, and spent the rest of his life in prison until he died in a hospital ward.

Being an advocate for a client is a privilege. Whether the client be popular or loathed, the lawyer's job as advocate is the same – to represent the client zealously in the pursuit of justice. Regardless of the case outcome, the pursuit of justice more than justifies the effort.

ABOUT THE AUTHOR

Jerry H. Summers is a practicing attorney in Chattanooga, Tennessee. Since beginning the practice of law in 1966, Summers has served as an assistant district attorney, a municipal judge, and in private practice. Except for seven years, between the ages of seven and fourteen when he lived in St. Petersburg, Florida, Summers has lived his entire life in Chattanooga, Tennessee.

He has argued cases before the United States and Tennessee Supreme Court and has been involved in numerous landmark decisions in both civil and criminal law.

His peers in the legal profession have elected him to membership in the International Academy of Trial Lawyers, American College of Trial Lawyers, International Society of Barristers, American Board of Trial Advocates, American Board of Criminal Lawyers, and he has been selected every year since 1983 as one of the Best Lawyers in America, in both personal injury and criminal law. By an unsolicited vote of the lawyers of Tennessee, he has consistently been selected as one of the "Best 100 Lawyers in Tennessee" and "Mid-South Super Lawyers."

Summers' philanthropy and community service has been honored by civic, educational, and professional organizations. Orange Grove Center and the Chattanooga Bar Association have both honored him as philanthropist of the year. In 2007, Central High School selected him as a distinguished alumnus at its Centennial Celebration. In 2014, Summers was designated as the Distinguished Alumnus at the University of the South at Sewanee and in 2016, he was named by the University of Tennessee at Knoxville as a distinguished alumnus.

This is Jerry Summers' eighth published book. His first, THE TURTLE AND THE LAWYER, released in 2014, is an attempt to thank those individuals and entities that have helped him in life and to suggest respectfully that the reader do the same. His second book, published in 2016, is a biography of the controversial life of Judge Raulston Schoolfield titled RUSH TO JUSTICE?: TENNESSEE'S FORGOTTEN TRIAL OF THE

CENTURY – SCHOOLFIELD 1958. In its sequel, *SCHOOLFIELD: OUT OF THE ASHES,* he completes the life story of the controversial jurist.

Summers' fourth book, *WE CALLED HIM COACH,* is about his football coach in high school, Stanley J. Farmer. Book number five, *ONE SHOT SHORT,* covers the 1957-1958 basketball team that lost the Tennessee State Championship by one point. The sixth book, *TENNESSEE TRIVIA NO. 1,* is a compilation of articles printed in the *Chattanooga Times Free-Press* and *Chattanoogan.com* website and deals with trivia in the State of Tennessee. Book seven, *TRI-STATE REFLECTIONS,* also a compilation of trivia articles, covers significant events in Tennessee, Alabama, and Georgia. It is important to point out that while this seventh book includes the story of the Leo Frank case, the other side of the story is covered in a subsequent article published on November 21, 2021, in *Chattanoogan.com.*

Minion Pro on LSI 50# Archival White
Type and Design by Karen Paul Stone